THE

REIMAGINED

Sustainable spaces
created with joy

HOME

NICOLE GRAY

Quadrille

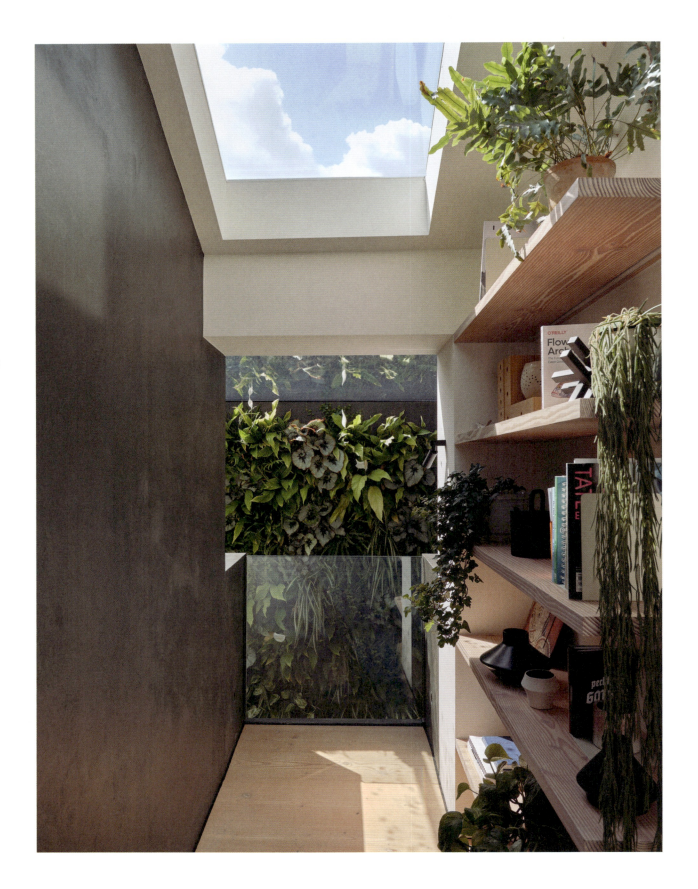

Introduction

Imagining how you want to live in a space is one of the most valuable forms of creative expression there is. It enables you to make choices – however big or small – that are authentic to you, your family and your circumstances.

Over the years, we have imagined our homes in myriad ways. This is mainly thanks to the abundance of information and tools at our disposal, including advancements in building materials, technology, online shopping, social media and the increased transparency of production lines allowing for better-informed decisions. From large-scale projects such as remodelling, refurbishing and expanding when budgets allow, to minimal interventions such as adding artwork and textiles, we now have more options than ever to define our spaces.

But what we require from our homes has evolved. No longer solely spaces to fulfill our basic needs of eating, drinking, bathing, sleeping and relaxing , home now needs to accommodate our heightened environmental awareness, shifting family structures, and renewed focus on our emotional and physical health. This book explores the concept of a home that embodies such principles. One that encourages us to push the envelope of design convention; to reimagine our spaces in ways that not only cater for our needs now, and those of the environment, but also speak to these into the future.

Whether accommodating a multi-generational family, adapting for age or illness, carving out space to run a business, or creating opportunities for biodiversity to thrive, the reimagined home is one that integrates thoughtful design that goes beyond simply adding a loft extension or installing a heat pump. Instead, it focuses on the exciting opportunities to be had when we reconceive how to live within a space, both now and for the years to come; a multiplicity of details that elevate the everyday and the exploration of extraordinary domestic architecture that enhance our living experience for the healthier and happier.

The inspiring homes of the 16 creatives featured within this book encapsulate what it means to live in such a reimagined way. Many were born out of necessity, or a series of practical considerations: limited budgets, growing families, commitment to reduce their carbon footprint or retirement. Although each of these spaces offers an infinite variety of ideas and designs for what it means to create a truly reimagined home, they all present a joyous and inspiring buffet of tips for you to create consciously and revel in the unexpected while planning for future flexibility.

For some, such as the Balinese *limasan* of ceramicists and designers Marcello and Michela, and the Victorian London townhouse of lifestyle entrepreneur Kate Blower, a reimagined space centres around fusing the past with the present, with traditional materials and building techniques used to construct contemporary living spaces that also give back to the environment.

For others, like the warehouse conversion of ceramicist Shelley Simpson in New South Wales, and the pocket-sized Margate apartment of interior designer Sophie van Winden, colour with a conscience is fundamental to their design ethos, and their homes are an extension of that.

But there are also houses at the other end of the spectrum, such as the converted *masseria* belonging to florist Kally Ellis in Puglia, where the palette is rooted in the natural world, or the Brooklyn townhouse of interior designer and sculptor Lyndsay Caleo and Fitzhugh Karol, where layers of reclaimed materials give the space a tactile homespun quality.

More than a handful of these spaces also challenge the expectation of what it means to live in today's modern world, eschewing the accessibility of baked-in software for our homes and the convenience of mass-produced materials, in favour of reclaimed 'natural' materials and fostering a deeper connection to nature that enables the residents to live a relatively unplugged lifestyle without sacrificing creativity.

The Reimagined Home is divided into four overarching chapters designed for you to dip into at every stage of your creative journey: 'Future-proof' presents strategies for adapting homes to meet the evolving needs of their occupants, from shifting work and family dynamics to the exploration of traditional building techniques that help prevent decay. 'Regenerative Design' explores the use of sustainable materials and practices that actively contribute to biodiversity, wellbeing and environmental health. 'Reuse, Rethink, Reinvent' highlights creative ways to refresh existing spaces, showing how to transform what is already there into something unique. 'Conscious Sourcing' focuses on blending preloved, vintage and contemporary pieces to create a meaningful and authentic home that is true to the lifestyles and values of its residents.

Together, these chapters aim to provide a concise guide to designing enduring, adaptable spaces that showcase sustainable design in all of its forms

This is not designed to be another 'how-to guide' for sustainable living, however, or even one that provides a definitive answer to the question of what we should do with our homes. Rather, this book is intended to spark the imagination of what we *could* do if we viewed the home as an extension of ourselves, our personality and the environment around us. It is a resource pool of suggestions for you to garner inspiration from. And, hopefully, elicit joy from in the process.

To everyone who contributed to these pages, thank you for sharing your stories and for taking this leap of faith with me. It's a privilege to showcase spaces that champion the joy and transformative power of a reimagined home.

A future-proofed home is one that ensures the long-term needs and living patterns of the occupants, focusing on variables such as comfort, practicality, accessibility, energy use and adaptability. Situated within the broader context of housing shortages, the rising cost of living, an ageing population and the increasingly blurred lines between work and home life, this form of living is becoming progressively important as social frameworks continue to shift.

Investing in multipurpose furniture is an easy and affordable way to start future-proofing your home. Think coffee tables with added storage, bunk beds for when the kids get older, a dining table that extends and storage units on wheels so that you can move them out of the way. Such an idea is seen in a renowned ceramicist's Australian warehouse, where modular walls have been placed on wheels to be easily reconfigured for business meetings, events and family time, depending on the occasion.

Bigger changes to living arrangements include retrofitting – improving insulation and airtightness through structural changes such as generating your own energy supply via a smart meter or installing solar PV (photovoltaic) panels on the roof – or finding innovative solutions to live off the land, such as in the Australian home of a kids' wear designer, where a septic tank powered by a 'worm farm' breaks down organic waste (including food) while producing fertilizer to feed the surrounding agriculture. Such additions may be costly in the short term, but easier and cheaper to run while distributing energy evenly throughout the home in the long term.

Opting for sustainable materials and traditional building techniques that help prevent decay and condensation may take longer, but is another way to fortify the health of your home and its occupants for years to come. In the sensitive holiday-home renovation of a renowned florist, traditional materials such as clay blocks and Travertino – a type of limestone formed by mineral deposits – along with walls made from fragments of earthenware, have been used to retore her dilapidated *agriturismo* back to its former glory.

The resounding thread that weaves throughout each of the spaces featured within this chapter is the core belief that future-proofing is about more than ticking items off a checklist for the home. It is about creating and preserving a personal space tailored to you.

Future-proof

Restoring a modernist marvel with
era-sensitive care

Renovating any home can be daunting, but it's rare that one finds oneself renovating an iconic building, let alone receiving the blessing of the original architect. Yet that is the situation that Katie Brannaghan, founder of online kids' boutique Hipkin, her husband Ian and their two daughters, Milla and Yvie, found themselves in when they purchased the Fender House in Victoria's Mount Martha.

Split over six levels and designed in 1973 by 'the wonder kid' of modernist architecture, Karl Fender (now co-founder of Fender Katsalidis, whose accolades include the Eureka Tower and Tasmania's Museum of Old and New Art), the space was a dream project but also one that raised the design stakes. 'Nothing encapsulates the seventies quite like the Fender House,' says Brannaghan of the famous property designed by a 23-year-old Fender for an eccentric local.

Karl Fender was a protégé of the late Robin Boyd, Australia's most influential post-war architect, who had a fervent dislike for the plague of bungalows rapidly sprawling across the country in the 1970s. Boyd made a name for himself by making the style of architecture traditionally reserved for the rich and famous – think Elvis Presley's house in Palm Springs – accessible and affordable to all. Tradesmen bought Boyd's floor plans for a few dollars back in the 1940s and created partially prefabricated family homes made from local materials that incorporated the modernist sensibilities of large windows and gardens that merged the indoors and outdoors. 'Most of these buildings have since been knocked down due to the rise in demand for subdivided homes,' explains Brannaghan. The Fender House – which follows Boyd's modernist design sensibilities – is among the remaining few of its style left standing.

When the couple first moved in, however, the house was falling apart. 'There was termite damage everywhere, asbestos, leaks and rot,' recalls Brannaghan. But underneath, the bones of the space – original wood panelling, high ceilings and vast double-storey windows – had great potential. The Slim Aarons-esque pool outside, although in disrepair, sealed the deal. 'It was sinking in on itself at the time but had all the trademarks of old-school Hollywood,' she says.

Previous inhabitants of the space had altered the original design with fixtures and fittings reminiscent of the 1990s and early 2000s. 'It was completely at odds with the history,' says Brannaghan, who made it her mission to strip the space back to its original bones using materials, furniture and furnishings circa 1973 – the way Karl Fender initially envisioned it. 'Ultimately we wanted to meld the past and the future together,' says Brannaghan. 'For the house to look forward while also looking back.'

Sourcing era-appropriate furniture and sustainable materials that were also sensitive to the house was no easy feat, but Brannaghan was determined to source the same building materials that would have originally featured in Fender's design. 'They used to have specific types of wood slats back then, in sizes that no longer exist in modern architecture,' she explains. This required the sourcing of a specialist who could replicate the original aesthetic using timber, which now traverses the ceilings of each level of the home and provides a rich patina throughout.

Original architectural flourishes that were once hidden are now celebrated: painted bagged brick walls (an application that covers surfaces without concealing the irregularity and texture) in the lounge, hallway and teenage zones, built-in wooden cabinetry in the breakfast room, original porthole lights in the kitchen and restored 1970s lightboxes throughout. These sit alongside authentic technology from the era such as the original wall-mounted telephone and a record room on the ground floor where the pair spin vinyls at the weekend. Reggae and seventies classics such as José Feliciano are among the favourites. 'It's like living in a time capsule,' says Brannaghan.

Brannaghan's passion for sourcing natural materials and original furniture goes beyond merely decorative, however, and more towards purposeful design that can evolve with its occupants. 'We replaced all harmful plastics with durable materials such as timber, stone and terrazzo, and supplemented the original floors with an Australian hardwood,' she says. The couple also added a low-impact hydronic heating system, which is four times more energy efficient than a standard ducted system, and installed solar panels on the roof to help offset the household's energy use.

In the garden, an impressive eco-septic tank powered by a 'worm farm' breaks down organic waste and provides fertilizer-rich water to feed the surrounding agriculture, most of which was propagated using existing plants. The couple are also slowly but steadily landscaping the garden to include fruit and vegetable beds for the family to utilize now and in the future, with Ian drawing up plans to build a Binishell (a 1960s-style energy-efficient concrete dome) in the garden. 'The aim is to be completely off-grid within the next few years,' he says.

While leaning towards modernism, Brannaghan is also careful to avoid rooms feeling too stark by blending in a mix of warm tones and tactile textures. 'Ninety per cent of the furniture is second-hand,' she says about hero items such as the dining table and chairs in the breakfast room, found in an antique furniture store in North Melbourne, and the 'worn and torn' vintage B&B Italia sofas that Brannaghan reupholstered in tanned leather, in keeping with the feel of the house.

Modern touches such as the chartreuse-green carpet – 'it's 100 per cent wool, so hardy, but soft underfoot' – that runs the length of the space and looks as if it has always been there, is another good example. Despite builders thinking it looked like an 'indoor lawn,' it has since spawned several copycat renditions on Instagram, with neighbours and visitors slyly calling in similar fabric swatches. The green of the carpet is complemented by the plethora of easy-to-maintain plants such as golden barrel cacti, dracaena trifasciata (mother-in-law's tongue), yuccas, succulents, palms, devil's ivy and monstera, which populate nooks throughout. 'They fit with the period while also helping to purify the air,' explains Brannaghan.

Of course, meeting the man responsible for such a space was the icing on the cake. 'Karl Fender paid us a visit after seeing the renovation journey on Instagram,' says Brannaghan. He arrived on the doorstep armed with his original drawings and floor plans (his hand-drawn picture of the house now takes pride of place on the wall above the fireplace) and bestowed his approval on the sensitive restoration. 'Turns out a lot of the renovations we carried out closely mirrored the original design, which was an amazing accolade.'

May the party never end.

13

Katie Brannaghan

The home bar in the music room is always stocked for weekend parties. Music ranges from Northern Soul to Brit Pop, Country and early 1980s hip hop. Hard-wearing 1970s style terrazzo flows throughout the high-traffic areas on the ground floor to the poolside.

The main bedroom is located on the ground floor in honour of the original early 1970s layout, and has its own private access to the pool area. Original bagged brick walls and joinery form the backdrop. The blue aluminium bed was made locally.

Brannaghan rebuilt the original rotting cabinetry with new timber joinery stained to match the original panels. Vintage Le Creuset pots and ceramics collected over years feature throughout.

The staircase is original, with stairs re-clad in a chartreuse woolen carpet.

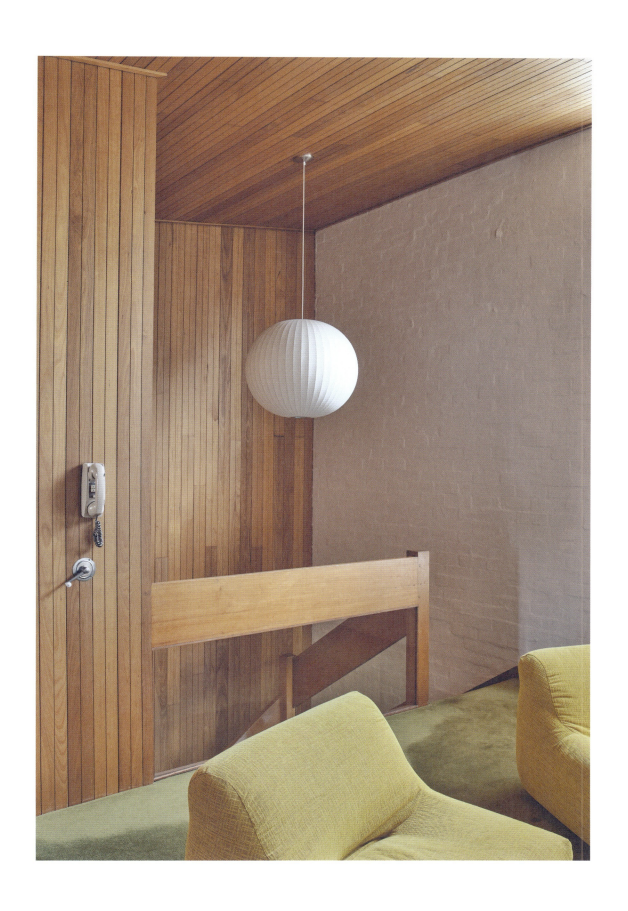

Describe your style in three words.
Modernist. Nostalgic. Colourful.

What does sustainability mean to you?
Using durable materials that will stand the test of time and avoiding contributing to landfill at all costs.

What are your top four tips for creating a reimagined home?
> Let the original features of the property, such as bare brick walls, inform the design and find ways to let them shine through.

> Bad design can be just as expensive as good design, so, where possible, don't scrimp on the pieces that bring you joy.

> Let natural materials take centre stage against a neutral backdrop where possible. It will help them stand out.

> Don't listen to the builders! Go with your gut on materials, finishes and colours that feel right for you in your space.

Who or what are your inspirations in terms of sustainable design?
It sounds corny but Karl Fender. He built houses using local materials made by local tradesmen; nothing was imported back then because it couldn't be. The design was better.

What triggers your creativity?
Proportion: seeing how things sit and work together to make each element better.

Your home makes you feel . . .?
Happy. Inspired.

What interior item couldn't you live without?
My stereo. It's a 1960s classic hi-fi with speakers.

Paint colour of choice?
Builder's white! It allows all of the textures, materials, colours and artwork in the house to sing.

Tell me something nobody knows about your home.
The previous eccentric owner used our bedroom as an office for his illegal bookmaking business. The office had a glass door so that he could see the police coming. He got raided a few times and used to eat all of his illegal betting slips before the police got through the door. They eventually caught him and sent him to jail. He was a character.

Finish the sentence: a considered home should be . . .
Somewhere that makes you feel good.

Inside a 16th-century agriturismo
revived with tradition

When you take on a derelict property in rural Italy – one with crumbling walls and parts of the roof missing – you need courage, vision and the interiors acumen to make it into a beautiful home. Luckily, as founder and former managing director of McQueens Flowers, these are skills that Kally Ellis has in spades.

What you will find when stepping through the threshold of Ellis's Puglian holiday home and rental accommodation – a joint business venture with actor, author and gardening enthusiast Charlie Higson – is a home that celebrates light, natural materials and antique finds to produce a vernacular that is as elegant as it is sustainably led.

'Kally' is the shortened version of Ellis's Greek birth name, Kalliope, and many of the nearby town and village names – Calimera, Gallipoli, Monopoli – also originated from Greece. So when it came time to name the house, 'it seemed apt to stick with this theme and felt more personal to use my name,' explains Ellis of the 16th-century fortified farmhouse now known as Masseria Kalliope. 'Masserias were tall, solidly built, traditional Italian farm estates,' says Higson, whose own masseria is located across the way. 'During the Middle Ages, they protected farmers from raiders who would plunder the Italian coastline from the Adriatic Sea. They were battle-hardy properties, remnants of which are still visible, from the thick stone walls to the high window look-out points.'

Kalliope is what is referred to as an agriturismo – a development where guests can stay and experience locally grown food and culture without negatively impacting the surrounding countryside. 'It also supports the development of rural areas by investing money back into the community,' says Ellis, who has used the surrounding fields to plant produce authentic to the region such as chicory, fennel, courgettes, aubergine, peppers, beans, potatoes and tomatoes. 'Humble ingredients that are easy to cook and taste delicious,' she says. Following the olive tree disease caused by spittlebugs that swept through the region several years ago, Higson has also replanted disease resistant olives in the hope that more trees will grow, along with new hemp and fig trees. 'We want to create an environment that will continue to sustain us long into the future,' says Ellis.

Photovoltaic cells have been installed along the roof of the accommodation blocks (unlike solar panels, PV cells don't rely on direct sunlight to work), with Ellis restoring the original well to help irrigate surrounding crops and supply the home with water. 'I love that every time I turn the tap on, I know the water is coming from our own land,' she says. Aquifers dating back 'millennia' are located underneath the wells and act as important buffers against drought. 'The Mediterranean climate relies on heavy rain in the winter which soaks down through the ground and fills up the aquifers so that come summer, the plants can live off the water reserve,' explains Higson – something which has become vital to the land since the rapid rise of global warming.

The space had been uninhabited since the 1950s ('the locals often tell us that they played in the empty rooms as kids,' says Ellis), before she and Higson took the plunge to buy it together in 2019 and convert it to a holiday home and rental. 'It was an Italian ruin,' says Ellis of the original three separate blocks that make up the property, most of which were crumbling, overgrown or dilapidated. 'There were no doors, windows, flooring, electricity or plumbing – everything had to be built from the ground up,' she says.

The main block, however, which now comprises the living room, kitchen and dining room, was mostly intact. 'It had these incredible stone vaulted ceilings,' recalls Ellis. 'As soon as I saw them, I was sold.' Another historical footnote of the property is that it used to be a raisin farm. 'Pasulo is the name of the surrounding area and also means raisin in the local dialect,' says Ellis. 'The raisins – made on the land from local grapes – were dried on the roof and swept down through the holes at the top of these amazing, vaulted ceilings when ready to eat or sell.'

Several of the original stone fireplaces also remained intact, along with alcoves (affectionately dubbed 'niches' by Ellis) that the previous inhabitants used to display their treasures and religious artefacts. Ellis now uses them to quietly layer her own treasures in the form of terracotta jugs, pots, bowls and urns in strikingly simple yet captivating shapes. 'Design doesn't have to be complicated to look good,' she says.

From the pots collected from markets and travels over many years and now brimming with wild foliage, to the time-worn dressers and consoles, almost nothing is new. In the dining room, a generously proportioned table – always prepped for Italian-style family meals – was made by an ex-model-maker-turned-carpenter friend of Ellis, Jamie Bowering (he made the Batmobile for the 1989 Batman movie starring Michael Keaton), using slabs of oak that Ellis found at a reclamation yard. In the living room, there is a large French mirror brought from Ellis's Norfolk home and a wooden coffee table 'gem' that she found while scouring the flea market in nearby Lecce. Alongside her vintage finds, Ellis has also made room for future family heirlooms, including the wrought-iron beds featured in the accommodation block, with finials dating back to the 19th century that Ellis unearthed and bought for a 'song' in a local antique warehouse ('I thought I was being really savvy, until I discovered the price to have them stripped back and reconditioned'), and the show-stopping, mermaid-base console table sourced from a local bric-a-brac warehouse called Tutto Usato (translated as 'Everything Used'.)

Ellis's inclination towards exquisite craftsmanship extends to the building materials used throughout the renovation. The kitchen counters, for example, are made from locally sourced Travertino (a type of limestone formed by mineral deposits), which creates a natural 'marbling' effect typical of this region of Italy. The masseria floors, originally used for housing farming animals, were rebuilt by local architectural practice Cubo, who installed underfloor blocks similar to those used by the Romans to facilitate air flow. 'They allow this type of building to "breathe",' explains Higson.

The second block, which was 'partially dilapidated' with one half of the roof intact and the other side a gaping void, was rebuilt in a mirror image, using traditional clay blocks made locally by hand, with walls rendered using traditional Pietra Leccese, stone from the local region made from fragments of earthenware to keep out moisture. From a distance, the stones look a lot like breezeblocks, but upon closer inspection, one can see traces of ancient fossils embedded in the mixture. 'The hardness and resistance of the stone, once extracted, increases over time, and takes on an amber colour similar to that of honey,' says Ellis of the result.

It's calming and captivating in equal measure; a sentiment that can be applied to the whole house.

Large urns and pots collected by Ellis from local flea markets are used as decoration throughout the home. In the summer they are filled with wild foliage from the surrounding land and structural branches in winter.

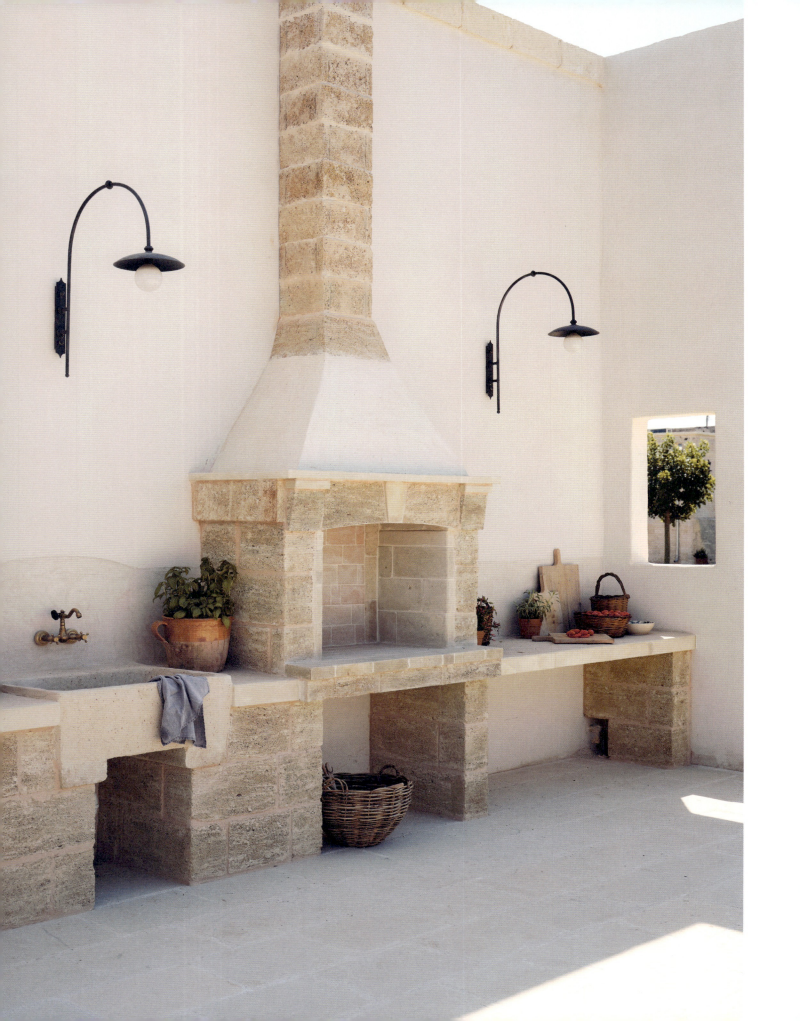

The outdoor kitchen is made from
opus signinum, a traditional waterproof
building material originally used in ancient
Rome to protect buildings from dampness.
It is made of pieces of broken pot, tile
and brick. Ancient aquifers are located
beneath the restored well that supplies
the masseria with water whilst feeding the
surrounding agriculture.

The original stone-vaulted ceiling featured in the open-plan living and dining space honours the property's history as a crypt during the First World War. The dining table, handmade by Ellis's carpenter using discarded slabs of oak, is decorated with organic linens sourced locally and Ellis's own collection. The pendant light was a salvage-yard find. The terracotta jugs were collected over years.

The handmade chequerboard floor tiles feature throughout
each of the bedrooms in tones reflective of the surrounding
landscape. The wrought-iron bed is from a local antique
market. Ellis stripped and reconditioned it and furnished it
with a locally made ticking mattress and organic linens.

Original niches feature throughout the masseria and are used by Ellis to display her vast collection of terracotta jugs, pots and vases collected over years. The console table is from a second-hand market.

Describe your style in three words.
Rustic. Classic. Elegant.

What does sustainability mean to you?
Getting off-grid by growing your own fruit and vegetables and finding ways to harness the power of nature, such as solar or photovoltaic cells and wind turbines.

What are your top four tips for creating a reimagined home?
> Slow decorating; embrace traditional building techniques and materials where possible. The result will be worth it in the long term.

> Source bigger items such as furniture locally to avoid unnecessary shipping.

> Reinvest back into the community by hiring local tradesmen and craftsmen.

> Where possible, use what is around you. Nature is often an untapped resource and will instantly elevate a room.

Who or what are your inspirations in terms of sustainable design?
My children are my inspiration. They are the next generation and remind me to be considerate of the environment.

What triggers your creativity?
I'm a magpie – flea markets and antique shops are my stomping grounds – and I love the challenge of renovation and restoration. There's nothing more satisfying than finding something that has been sadly neglected and breathing new life into it. That is the spark that spurs me on creatively.

Your home makes you feel . . .
Safe.

What interior item couldn't you live without?
My large terracotta pots. I love them so much they feature in every room. They are beautiful on their own or full of foliage from the surrounding land.

Paint colour of choice?
Anything rich and creamy.

Tell me something nobody knows about your home.
This property used to be a crypt during the First World War. One of the locals dreamt that if they dug it up, they would find a statue of the Virgin Mary and it would end the war. Despite the local inhabitants descending on the property in their droves armed with spades, no such statue was found and they eventually had to fence off the property to stop them from digging it into the ground. It would make for a good film one day.

Finish the sentence: a considered home should be . . .
Functional, followed by beautiful.

The vibrant warehouse conversion honouring original materials

It takes creative vision and vim to imagine living in a gritty space that was once an industrial fruit factory. But for Shelley Simpson, founder of the vibrant ceramic table and homeware brand Mud Australia – much loved by the likes of Gwyneth Paltrow and Nigella Lawson – this unusual history only added to the appeal. Simpson lives on the converted upper floor of a vast double-brick warehouse located in the west of Sydney with husband James, son Spencer and Molly the Wheaten Terrier. The space also multifunctions as 'the mothership' for Mud, with one of the Mud shops and pottery studios located directly below. 'When I'm finished working, I just walk upstairs and I'm home,' smiles Simpson. It is the perfect blend of functionality and fun.

For Simpson, who fell in love with pottery in her 20s after discovering a kick wheel in her friend's garden shed, a warehouse home conversion located above the shop was an easy decision. 'We had outgrown our old studio space and needed more room to evolve our manufacturing process, as well as store the raw materials and finished products once fired,' she explains. The warehouse is also located just around the corner from their old studio and met with all of the couple's stipulations for a house project: the ability to create light, an open-plan layout to ensure optimal living, vast space downstairs to store materials and a beautiful space upstairs that could evolve with them as a family.

'When we first saw it, there was nothing in here,' says Simpson, gesturing around the 3,500 square metres of open living space. 'It was like living in a large brick box.' The couple could also hear tropical geckos living in the rafters – 'They must have migrated here in a bunch of bananas or pineapples and never left.' The first thing Simpson did was carve the space into separate areas. The bathroom, laundry room and dressing room were partitioned by three-quarter height walls, leaving a deliberate gap between them and the warehouse ceiling for fluidity between areas and to maintain an open-plan feel. Simpson also had several new internal walls placed on wheels, so they can be moved depending on the family's evolving needs. 'The modular walls allow us to change the main living and dining space to suit our lifestyle; whether it be hosting an intimate dinner for friends, family time or over a hundred people for a business event,' she says. 'It works on multiple levels.'

Despite the couple's interest in design, their home was not influenced by trends or the work of other designers, but rather created along with Mark Simpson and Damien Mulvihill, from DesignOffice, with whom Simpson had worked before. The brief was to keep it airy, maximize light and ensure it was also a versatile and functional space for work and leisure. Simpson also wanted to embrace the existing fabrics and materials, rather than board or paint over them. Having designed previous Mud retail spaces, the architects were familiar with Simpson's aesthetic and her desire to evolve the style of the space while maintaining the original essence.

'They took inspiration from the existing steel frame and went from there,' recalls Simpson. Original features remain intact: exposed brick and pipework, wooden floorboards and steel frames were allowed to sing with minimal interference. 'I wanted to stay true to the heritage,' explains Simpson, with the exposed ceiling beams, insulation materials and original scuff marks and signage from the property's past life becoming a design feature in themselves.

Unsurprisingly, Simpson had very specific ideas as to how the kitchen should look. The bench measures eight metres long with a twelve-metre back bar area, providing an eye-catching yet practical space for team lunches and family meals. There are two closed-off bedrooms at one end, with bathrooms and dining rooms at the other end. 'The kitchen is where we all meet in the middle,' she says. It has also been known to transform into a team yoga studio, creative workshop and a Christmas lunch venue, complete with disco balls. 'The space makes all things possible because it is so expansive – with points to hang things from the ceiling, plants that can grow four metres high, and enough room for it to still feel like home.'

Indeed, despite the industrial heritage and layout, the space feels cosy, lived-in and warm, without veering into the over-decorative. There is nothing frilly or fussy here. Pieces are highly functional and designed to last. 'I would rather buy one well-made item than several disposable pieces,' she says of the handcrafted 'investment piece' corner sofa from BDDW that James got for his birthday several years ago. 'Some people invest in fast cars, for us it's a forever sofa,' says Simpson. The rest of the furniture, lovingly collected over many years, is a combination of design classics and modern touches: Serge Mouille lights, an E. Kold Christiensen PK61 coffee table and armchairs by German designer Horst Brüning, paired with heirloom items such as the baby grand piano that Simpson inherited from her mother.

Everything in Simpson's home is a movable feast, set against a framework of raw brickwork, natural woods and colourful jolts, such as the wall of statement artwork accumulated over years from friends and family – including pieces by Paul Worstead and James Gallagher – organic linens in vibrant shades and the handmade kitchen units covered in coloured Laminex (layers of sustainably sourced kraft paper saturated with resin and compressed at a high temperature for durability). A large burnt-orange painting depicting a bowl being made is displayed on one of the partitions with a smattering of Mud vases and vessels in complementing shades stacked throughout in cabinets, on consoles and on bedside tables. Nothing here is for 'display only'; everything is fit for purpose. 'I believe good design starts with function, followed by form and aesthetics,' says Simpson.

Sustainability is a resounding thread throughout. Not surprising, given Mud's carbon-neutral credentials (any emissions that can't be avoided such as international shipping and travel are offset with carbon credits) and tireless commitment to reducing waste within the industry. 'Responsible consumption starts with good design,' asserts Simpson about Mud's clay-recycling system that creates new pieces from 100 per cent waste material. Broken pieces, spills and trimmings are also recast and remixed to minimize landfill. Excess heat is diverted into the production studio through a pipe to dry moulds and products as naturally as possible.

Solar panels have been installed on the roof of the property and provide about a third of the power needs, and rainwater storage tanks have been added to clean materials in the studio. 'Even if you are renting, these elements will save you money in the long run and help future-proof your home,' Simpson says. The result is a spacious multifunctional loft that will continue to grow and evolve with its occupants. 'I wanted to create a home where the design choices had longevity and offered flexibility for our family and business needs,' affirms Simpson. A reminder that when thought goes into the installation and care of materials, little else is needed.

The pottery studio is positioned directly below the warehouse and allows Simpson to split her time between the office and home. Mud's zero-waste policy means that broken pieces and leftover trimmings are recast and remixed to create new ceramics. Pieces are dried using excess heat diverted from the home into the production studio.

The open-plan kitchen is the linchpin of the space with an 8-metre long bench that accommodates family mealtimes, Christmas parties and business meetings. The joinery was designed by DesignOffice and custom-made by joiners before being covered in Laminex, using FSC-approved paper from sustainably grown- forests and water-based resin.

In the dressing room, open wardrobes custom-made locally from plywood keep clothing and accessories to hand. The handmade rug is from B-corp-certified company, Armadillo. A vintage Murano glass chandelier is hung from the warehouse beams to bring a touch of 1920s glamour to an industrial space.

Describe your style in three words.
Whimsical. Timeless. Functional.

What does sustainability mean to you?
Buying better, not more. Within the business, it has had to become the first question when starting any project. What is the best type of kiln for energy saving? How do we recycle our trimmings? For me, sustainability isn't just a concept – it's a lifestyle that shapes every choice I make.

What are your top four tips for creating a reimagined home?
> Use high-quality materials and finishes that are made locally to avoid shipping.

> Choose well-made furniture that you will love for a long time and reupholster where possible.

> Utilize green energy methods like solar panels and recycle rainwater.

> Choose timeless styles and colours – try to avoid anything trend-led.

Who or what are your inspirations in terms of sustainable design?
The team here at Mud Australia is constantly inspiring me. My partner, James, especially helps me lift the bar. I think time, and turning 60, makes me realize that we're not here for long and we need to be mindful of how we're choosing to impact the planet with our decisions.

What triggers your creativity?
At the moment, for me, creativity is all about sustainability and what more can we do to reuse and repurpose.

Your home makes you feel . . .
Creative. Lucky.

What interior item couldn't you live without?
I have several! It would have to be our Vitsoe shelving, my Lobmeyr coupe and my organic linen bed sheets.

Paint colour of choice?
It used to be grey but now it is off-white. Farrow & Ball's Wimborne White is a favourite of mine. I was always told it's easier to change the colour of your drapes or cushions or a bright coloured piece of porcelain than to have your whole house repainted. Since then, I have opted for versatile shades that go with everything.

Tell me something nobody knows about your home.
I have an original hand-blown 1920s art deco Murano glass chandelier, previously owned by Fleur Wood, above my velvet pouffe in my dressing room.

Finish the sentence: a considered home should be . . .
Textural and reflective of your unique style.

A Victorian terrace retrofit for energy efficiency

What happens when you mix the brutalist architecture of the Barbican, the art-deco touches of the Chrysler building and the sculptural modernism of Donald Judd? The answer is The Judd, a converted Victorian terrace in Tottenham, North London.

Yet there is nothing to indicate to the casual passerby that a world inspired by such influences lies beyond the unassuming brick facade. Named primarily after the famous American post-war artist, Donald Judd, the house is like a living sculpture, with schemes, textures and shapes in much bolder flavours than the average Victorian terrace. 'The house is like a Tardis, completely different from what you would expect from walking in off the street,' says Patricia Lynch, a former furniture restorer, of the unusual home that she shares with partner Gwen Williams, a retired solicitor, and their Border Collie, Shep. 'We didn't want a bog-standard terrace-house renovation, we were looking to create something that was both beautiful to be in and functional to use.'

Having already lived in the space for more than twenty years, the couple's initial instinct had been to move out of London. However, the house, with its transport links and proximity to the hustle and bustle of London, persuaded them otherwise. 'It didn't make financial sense to move,' explains Williams. 'Not when we had already invested money with the addition of a side extension.' The motto 'don't move, improve' came into play, with the pair deciding to focus on future-proofing the existing house while driving the aesthetic in a new and exciting sustainable direction.

They enlisted the design prowess of Ewald Van Der Straeten, co-founder of the architectural firm Bradley Van Der Straeten (BVDS), to transform their space into a unique home in which they could enjoy retirement. 'We were inspired by the company's innovative reimagination of previous Victorian terraces,' says Lynch of the practice, who pride themselves on starting each project with a deep dive into the minutiae of the homeowners' needs. Undeterred by the narrow footprint of their traditional home, Lynch and Williams poured their wildest dreams into the design brief, citing iconic buildings such as the Barbican and Tate Modern as inspiration for the overall look and feel of the space.

The eureka moment, however, came in the form of '*Untitled 1963*', an abstract sculpture by Donald Judd that Lynch and Williams saw at an exhibition. They found themselves inspired by the pattern formation. The piece itself is minimal in feel but represents a concave space through the repetition of arched fins, a signature design feature that went on to inform the unique upside-down curved timber ceiling that came to define the ground floor extension, and which in turn became the springboard for every subsequent design choice made by BVDS for the space. 'It's apt that we called this space The Judd after Donald's work,' says Van Der Straeten. 'His influence can be seen throughout, from the geometric tactile surfaces to the upbeat colour palette.'

Choosing the right tones to uplift a classic Victorian space required a discerning eye, however. 'We didn't want the house to look "cartoony",' explains Van Der Straeten, 'so we steered clear of primary colours and instead focused on seemingly strange colour combinations that worked together.' In the kitchen, handcrafted wooden cabinets are painted in an earthy terracotta, the tone of which is reflected in the speckled finish of the sweetshop-like terrazzo countertops and clay flooring, with the lower units painted in a sharp mint for balance. In the main bedroom, a cocooning lilac hugs the walls, with a refreshing strip of pale blue preventing the scheme from straying into 'sugary'.

Echoing Judd's work, blue is a recurring theme throughout the house, with variations running from the powder blue of the bathroom tiles to the cool pastel of the main bedroom, through to the rich blue used for the timber lining in the loft space and the new cobalt concrete cladding that ripples across the eye-catching extension. It is Van Der Straeten's version of the 'red thread', which pulls the scheme together while keeping rooms distinctive.

Colour palette aside, the biggest challenge of the space was to create something that looked extraordinary, while at the same time delivering a future-proofed home that would be comfortable to live in and low-energy to run. English Victorian properties are 'notoriously leaky buildings, with low levels of thermal efficiency', says Van Der Straeten. BVDS took a 'fabric first' approach that focused on making the building as airtight and thermally efficient as possible. Due to the property already being a double-brick house with 'breathable' construction, the solution was to line the walls internally using cork insulation, finished with lime render, which provided a full thermal wrap for the property while still allowing moisture to escape through the walls.

To reduce waste, Van Der Straeten kept the original footprint of the space intact, taking away elements rather than adding them in. The downstairs was originally made up of three separate rooms: the kitchen, dining room and a miscellaneous middle room, which became a 'dumping ground' for the couple's stuff. 'We didn't use the space to its best capacity,' says Lynch. Van Der Straeten knocked through the dividing wall between the kitchen and middle space to make for an integrated dining/entertainment area while creating a seamless look-through to the garden. 'It increased the overall feeling of spaciousness without using large amounts of building materials,' he explains. All external walls, including the side wall of the previous extension, were fully retained for further waste reduction, and extra cork insulation was added.

The wow factor undoubtedly comes in the form of the eye-catching curved ceiling, made up of 19 timber 'fins' that create movement by casting pools of shadow and light across the floor and walls. 'It works with the playful nature of the house in a way that glass could not,' explains Van Der Straeten. Movement continues throughout in the form of the handmade geometric tiled wall in the entrance hallway – the 'backbone' of the house – and on the kitchen island. 'They bring texture, shape and rhythm to areas that would often be overlooked,' says Van Der Straeten.

One of the biggest environmentally led decisions the couple made was to install an air-source heat pump, which is located in the garden and helps heats the home by taking energy from the outside air. The electricity used to run the air-source heat pump is supplemented by power from photovoltaic panels (cells that convert sunlight into electricity) that have been installed on the roof. 'The results have been astonishing,' says Lynch. Before the renovation, gas and electricity bills were well above average for a house of these proportions, with figures dropping by 75 per cent on energy consumed following the works. 'It has completely changed how we utilize the space,' says Williams.

The result is a house that is so much more than the sum of its parts. It's a place where sustainability and style converge to create a home that makes its occupants very happy. 'We won't be moving anytime soon,' says Williams.

The rear view of the original side return extension is covered in corrugated blue concrete cladding, added by Van Der Straeten. The curved doorway mirrors the star of the space – the bespoke curved kitchen ceiling comprised of 19 timber fins. New windows and a large rooflight enable light to flow freely throughout whilst linking the indoors and out.

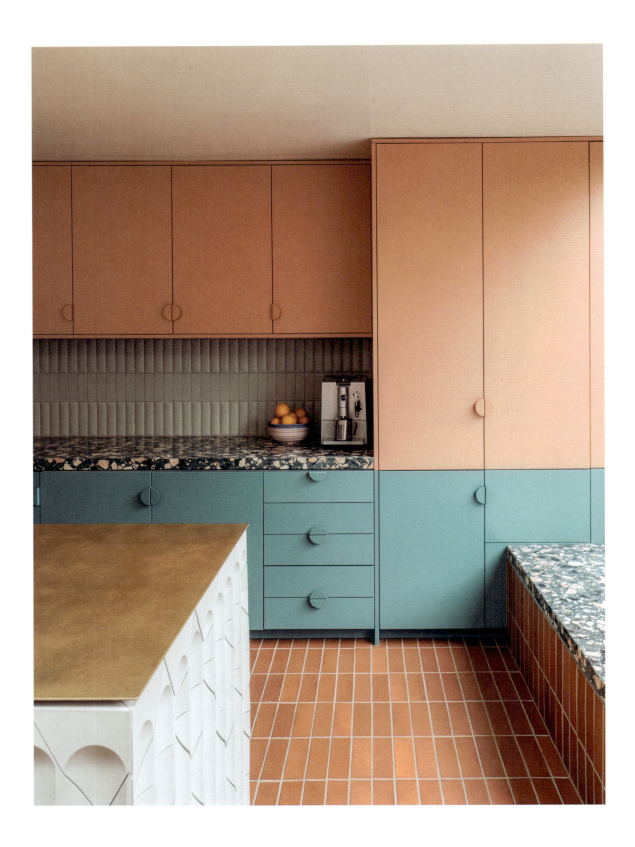

The kitchen cabinetry is painted in vibrant clay-based colours picked out from the surrounding terrazzo worktops. Brick tiles are continued up the lower half of the wall as durable skirting and reference the traditional flooring of Victorian kitchens. The kitchen island is clad in fluted three-dimensional concrete tiles topped with patina-rich brass.

The statement stairwell is doused in bright pink leading up to the loft and an impressive skylight. The shade was inspired by Mexican architect Luis Barragán.

In the home office, the lower half of the wall is made from fluted Valchromat, a wood fibreboard coloured using organic dyes, bonded together with resin.

The first floor main bathroom was turned into a spacious shower room, with handmade terrazzo tiles decorated with glass and marble fragments, and brushed brass fixtures and fittings.

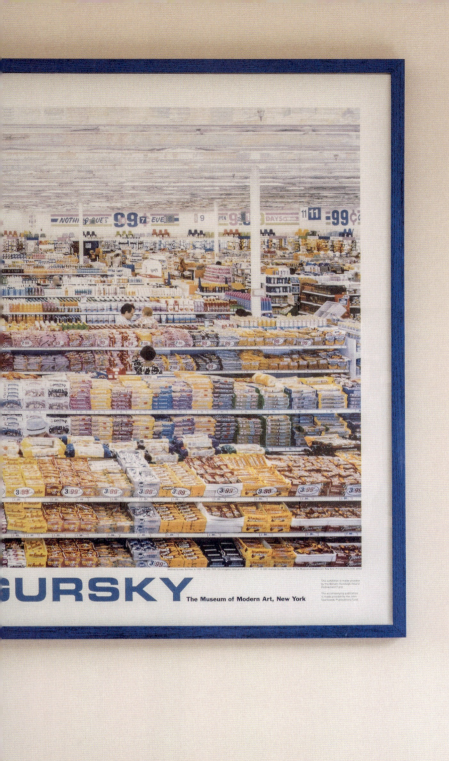

Describe your style in three words.
Colourful. Comfortable. Functional.

What does sustainability mean to you?
Minimizing waste as much as possible. If something still works how it is supposed to, why replace it?

What are your top four tips for creating a reimagined home?

> Incorporate elements of vibrant colour throughout, even if it's initially through accents such as floorboards or skirting.

> Surround yourself with items that work. There is no point in having something beautiful if it isn't practical or built to last.

> Being closer to nature is paramount. Rearrange your furniture so that the desk or armchair is positioned by a window.

> Have fewer items on surfaces. It will help calm the mind.

Who or what are your inspirations in terms of sustainable design?
I'm an avid fan of the television programme *Grand Designs*. As an ex-furniture restorer, I'm always on the lookout for ideas on how to utilize what is already in existence and find that the show offers many innovative solutions.

What triggers your creativity?
Gadgets. We like to dismantle simple objects and put them back together, it helps keep the mind curious and gets the creative cogs whirring.

Your home makes you feel . . .
Joyous.

What interior item couldn't you live without?
The Grand Repos Chair by Antonio Citterio. We've had it for years. It's in the living room where we like to read.

Paint colour of choice?
Sapling by Earthborn. We have used it in the hallway.

Tell me something nobody knows about your home.
We deliberately decided not to renovate or decorate the exterior of the house, so that when people step inside, the design takes them completely by surprise.

Finish the sentence: a considered home should be . . .
Beautiful and practical.

Patricia & Gwen

If sustainability is about mitigating problems, regenerative design is about repairing the damage already caused to our environment, creating opportunities for biodiversity and removing carbon from the atmosphere, while at the same time striving to create beautiful homes with longevity at the core.

Homes that are designed using materials drawn directly from nature such as wood, hemp, limestone and bamboo, will create a closed-loop relationship that works *with* the environment rather than against it. Whether it's designing and making your furniture from reclaimed materials, as seen in the Brooklyn home of an interior design duo, or incorporating nature-sensitive infrastructure that gives back to the environment, as in the Bali home of a sculptor and ceramicist, regenerative design encourages us to seek new and inventive ways for the human and natural world to coexist.

Regeneration is not only about renewable building materials, however; it is also about embracing biophilic design by incorporating natural elements such as vegetation and natural light into residential spaces. It goes beyond mere aesthetics to create environments that support our emotional well-being. Choices such as growing our own fruit and vegetables, 'rewilding' our gardens and bringing plants inside help us tap into our innate connection with nature and harness the health benefits.

Such ideas show us what is possible when we elevate the ordinary to the unexpectedly brilliant, redesigning our homes in unconventional and exciting ways that not only benefit the environment, but also our wellbeing.

Regenerative Design

A modern Balinese limasan
shaped by nature

For husband-and-wife team Marcello Massoni and Michela Foppiani, their home in the tropical landscape of Ubud, which they share with their three teenage sons, Martino, Metello and Mario, and labradoodle Mimmo, is at the foundation of everything they do.

Almost two decades ago, they moved to Ubud from Piacenza, a small town near Milan, to further establish and nurture their hand-thrown pottery brand, Gaya Ceramic. Fast-forward 25 years and Gaya is a leading design destination that boasts a team of over 100 local craftsmen who form, fire and glaze their one-of-a-kind ceramics and lighting range, with prestigious clients including Armani/Casa and Bulgari Hotels.

Ceramics are hand-thrown using a variety of natural materials such as porcelain, raku clay and stoneware and, as such, everything has a bespoke, one-off quality. 'We also use every scrap of leftover clay to help minimize waste while creating something new,' says Marcello. 'Until we open the kiln, we don't know exactly how a piece will look, but that is the joy of creation.'

Considered design is not the cherry on the cake for the couple, rather it is at the core of every decision they make. Marcello left his career path in economics and politics to pursue one made of clay. 'I fell in love with Miki and how she transformed simple clay into something special with purpose, longevity,' he recalls. Michela now designs all of the collections at Gaya, with Marcello overseeing production to ensure that each piece is aligned with their overarching creative vision: intuition, inspiration, craft and love.

Their home, located in the middle of a rice field framed by a jungle and a creek, is not only a testament to the power of their creativity but also a physical extension of Gaya; humble in its vernacular structure with a limited range of natural materials on repeat throughout, which not only bear a deep connection to the surrounding landscape, but are built to last and minimize impact on the environment. In the living and dining space, a stainless-steel kitchen designed by the couple is framed by glass walls and teak columns that both insulate and support the space while allowing uninterrupted vistas over the landscape, with concrete countertops and flooring throughout that absorbs heat from the sun during the day and stores it for cool nights while also providing a durable design solution in high-traffic areas. 'We love the strength of wood and stone, coupled with the fragility of ceramics and glass, and the patina they acquire over time,' says Michela.

The design is true to the people who live in this space, as well as to the heritage of the building. Two large *limasan* pavilions – traditional Javanese architectural verandas, made out of solid teak – supported by columns and topped with terracotta roof tiles and bamboo skin for insulation-were sourced locally, built by hand and now house the alfresco dining/entertainment area. The couple also enlisted the help of Italian firm BAMM ARCHITECTS to build a series of simple blocks around the pavilions to form the guest room, primary bedroom and children's rooms, informing an aesthetic that is part-industrial, part-traditional, and steeped in history while also setting its sights on the future.

The connection to the surrounding environment goes beyond the materials used. To the naked eye, the house itself appears to emerge from the landscape, an idyllic notion reinforced by the open-plan layout and lack of internal walls. 'It is boundless freedom,' explains Michela. All spaces seem to stem from the open kitchen and dining area, which reduces the distance between utility functions, cutting construction costs. The omission of walls also ensures this space can be easily reconfigured to accommodate future owners. The bedrooms are the only enclosed spaces in the house (to protect from wild animals), with all other areas leading seamlessly into the outdoors. In the en-suites, 'open-air' showers are enclosed within stone walls and framed by plants for privacy. A hand-painted *trompe l'œil* mural, based on the work of 20th-century artist Henri Rousseau, wraps and zones the kitchen area, with a cacophony of oversized plants further punctuating the space with the vibrant scale and drama of the outdoors.

Despite the abundance of robust materials and tactile layers throughout, the couple has left deliberate gaps throughout the scheme to allow space for what truly matters to them: an intuitive mix of the old and new. Treasured finds include a traditional decorative bull head – often found within vernacular homes in the Toraja Sulawesi region of Indonesia – hanging above a dresser in the entranceway, a vibrant green painting, made by a local artist entitled 'Learning To Fly' that reminds the couple of their sons who will soon leave the nest, and a small ceramic Chinese horse, both displayed on the statement gallery wall full of pieces collected from friends and family over the years.. These are paired with the occasional design wild-card that keeps the mood jovial: the large wooden tiger that guards the veranda, a ceramic arm made by Michela and moved around the home as a fun vignette, and the Pinocchio puppet, made from clay by Marcello, that adds a playful touch to a gallery wall shelf. 'We have a thousand small things,' says Michela, 'each one with a story to tell.'

The entrance to the downstairs bathroom is a case in point, adorned with handmade ceramic leaves designed by Michela to reflect the tropical foliage surrounding the property. Leftover curtains from a project the couple worked on in Sydney are embroidered with the shape of ceremonial Balinese rice cakes and repurposed as an oversized headboard in the main bedroom. 'Our work always feeds back into the home,' explains Marcello, gesturing to the abundance of stylishly stacked ceramic pieces from Gaya displayed in cabinets and on shelves. 'There is no such thing as ceramic "failures" at the studio. If we can't sell it or it doesn't work out the way we planned, we usually take it home or upcycle it.' In that sense, the home is ever evolving. Always building on itself.

There is an essence of magic here that is hard to resist. 'We enjoy the open feel of the house, the connection to nature, sense of community and luxurious width of space,' concludes Marcello. It all adds up to something a little bit different while maintaining respect for heritage, culture, tradition and the land.

In the open-plan living and dining block, rectangular glass-and-iron walls enclose a hard-wearing, stainless-steel kitchen. A jungle trompe l'oeil mural wraps the walls in nature and further blurs the line between the indoors and out.

Ceramics feature in abundance throughout, from cabinets full of
handmade tableware to glazed wall coverings and tiles used as
practical hard-wearing 'carpets' in semi-outdoors areas.
The guest bathroom entrance, located in the open-plan living
room, is adorned with ceramic leaves made by Michela.

85

Marcello & Michela

The couple's interest in simple, honest, natural materials and commitment to zero-waste is reflected in the space. Shelves throughout are stacked with past and present ceramic creations that were originally made at Gaya before being repurposed at home.

The bedrooms are the only enclosed blocks in the home, with visitas of the landscape visible through iron-framed windows. The headboard and connecting side tables are made out of concrete, with the top half clad in leftover curtain fabric from a previous Gaya project depicting traditional Balinese rice cakes.

Artwork acquired over years from friends and family are displayed on an expansive backdrop of blue glazed ceramic tiles framed by teakwood columns. The blue chair and footstool was designed and handmade by Marcello and Michela. A vintage 'Aladdin' shop sign forms the focal point.

Describe your style in three words.
Open. Free. Natural.

What does sustainability mean to you?
To balance our personal lifestyle with Mother Nature.

What are your top four tips for creating a reimagined home?
› Always avoid convention. Find ways to elevate the ordinary into the unexpectedly brilliant by creating something new from nothing or something old.

› Be respectful of nature and your surrounding environment. Where possible, try to link your design to the land, both in terms of the materials and the overall design aesthetic.

› Only surround yourself with things that you have an emotional attachment to. They will act as reminders of the different stages and memories of life.

› Work with the bones of the space you have: let heritage, layout and quirks of the space inform the design process.

Who or what are your inspirations in terms of sustainable design?
We love the work of architect Kengo Kuma, who integrates his buildings with their surroundings, emphasizing materials that reflect the local context and culture. He has an amazing ability to connect infrastructure with the landscape using simple and natural construction materials that are renewable, durable and long-lasting.

What triggers your creativity?
Almost everything. While in our work we create a lot of custom projects, we are often forced to explore aesthetics and practical fields that are not specifically ours. We are always on the lookout for new ideas and styles.

Your home makes you feel . . .
Connected to nature.

What interior item couldn't you live without?
Most probably our wooden tiger.

Paint colour of choice?
Anything with a green-grey gradient

Tell me something nobody knows about your home.
In our living room, just above our little green sofa, a couple of turtle doves have made their nest. They are part of our family now.

Finish the sentence: a considered home should be . . .
An expression of you and the future you want for your family. It is where you connect meaningfully with each other with no pretence.

Craftsmanship meets biophilic design in a Brooklyn brownstone

Certain aesthetics come to mind when one thinks of Brooklyn living: exposed brick, pipework and loft-style living rooms. But in the Park Slope home of husband-and-wife duo Lyndsay Caleo and Fitzhugh Karol, founders of The Brooklyn Home Company (TBHCo), biophilic shapes and natural finishes give an intentionally rejuvenating atmosphere to the four-storey brownstone where they live with their two children, Charlotte and 'Bay'.

It's a thread that weaves through their work, both at home and in the acclaimed residential projects carried out by TBHCo, which the pair co-run with Lyndsay's brother, Bill Caleo. Lyndsay spearheads the architectural design, Fitzhugh the artistic installations and handcrafted sculptures (often made out of reclaimed timber) and Bill the real estate. Together they are committed to creating spaces that champion a greener way of living through the use and reuse of raw materials that bear a close connection to the surrounding environment. 'When it comes to interior design, most of what you need already exists. You just need to utilize it,' says Lyndsay of the company's design philosophy.

The couple's home is a testament to this mantra – superfluous, mass-produced details filtered out in favour of fixtures, fittings and furniture that go beyond utility and embrace the craftsmanship behind each piece. Nothing here is cookie-cutter. Furniture is designed and handmade by Lyndsay and Fitzhugh and ranges from the mahogany shelves in the kitchen to the Sapele kitchen island, reclaimed mahogany coffee table and the couple's four-poster bed, carved by Fitzhugh 15 years ago from a beech tree that had toppled near Lyndsay's childhood home. Pieces are designed not only to last but to give back to the environment, with recyclable materials in the form of wood, stone and marble, sourced from previous renovations or nature, on repeat.

As such, subtle yet deliberate contours and curves feature throughout and link to the concept of biophilia, while breaking the stiff lines normally associated with a Brooklyn townhouse. Installation-esque artworks made by Fitzhugh act as further nods to silhouettes reflective of nature. In the living room, a large wall-mounted sculpture fashioned from leftover wood scraps overlaps symmetrically 'like a cluster of falling leaves' and creates a focal point above the fireplace. In the hallway hangs an arresting cobalt blue carved timber panel made by Fitzhugh when their daughter Charlotte was born; in the entrance hall sits a Totem-like structure carved from a felled tree that both intrigues and delights the senses. 'We aim to create emotional architecture,' says Lyndsay. 'When you enter into a space, the environment and architecture also enter you. How you build, what you build and the materials which we use to build – it all plays a role in how one feels within a space.'

The couple originally lived on the lower two floors of the property, which needed a lot of work following a fire in the 1980s, after which the space was left unoccupied for many years. Despite the damage and the couple having to rip out the majority of the existing elements, as they were unusable, there were still 'enough guts' of the original building left for them to preserve or salvage. The original fireplaces, plasterwork and staircase (although originally very rickety) remain intact, with other elements given a new lease of life elsewhere in the home.

The sofa, made out of some of the original ceiling beams, is a case in point. A barn door from Fitzhugh's family farm in New Hampshire is used as the sliding door in the bathroom. Bricks from the original building have also been repurposed as a retaining wall and planting beds in the garden. 'Our design is about using old materials in new ways,' explains Fitzhugh, as a testament to the couple's dedication to pieces that go full circle.

Throughout the renovation process, the couple made decisions that not only had a positive impact on the environment but also on the day-to-day health of people living in the space. Lyndsay's brother Bill suffers from severe asthma, a condition that was exacerbated by city life and inspired him to explore building materials that promote a cleaner way of living. The property is south-facing and the walls are naturally insulated with bricks, which results in minimal energy being used to heat and cool the property, promoting a higher quality of air indoors. This is reinforced by the handcrafted pieces, raw finishes and recyclable natural fibres used throughout that further cut down on harmful toxins.

The couple kept the structure of the original walls and only added windows in the kitchen to maximize light and let it flow freely. Light is also used as a medium throughout, set against Lyndsay's careful selection of unfussy neutral shades on the walls and floors that act as a blank canvas for Fitzhugh's creations and the interplay between raw materials. The light creates crescendos and moments of calm throughout. 'Nothing here jostles for attention,' says Lyndsay, 'everything is balanced by the natural movement of things.'

The lower basement and parlour floors were extended out another ten feet and the two upper floors converted into a contemporary duplex for the couple's growing family. The original parlour floor now houses the dining room and an open-plan kitchen that overlooks the rear garden, with the upper floors now consolidated to house the primary bedroom, kids' bedrooms and play space. The lower floor encompasses a guest bedroom and working studio space.

Despite the sprawling floor plan, townhouses in Brooklyn are narrow, an architectural trait that the couple have used to their advantage. 'We have a lot of height in Brooklyn,' explains Lyndsay, 'but not much square footage, so we wanted to make every inch count.' As such, storage is incorporated throughout, but in ways that eschew the formality of a traditional townhouse and instead take the opportunity to create playful pockets. In the kitchen, a lofted sleeping nook designed and built by the couple is positioned above an enclosed storage wall accessed by a wooden ladder. In the dining space, a narrow door conceals organic linens, while a hidden bookshelf in the sleeping nook captures the essence of childhood nostalgia for discovery and creative exploration, further fuelled by the series of arches and hideaways repeated on various scales throughout. 'Materials create moments that then create memories,' smiles Lyndsay.

It is this intrinsic sense of materiality that binds the space together, with any gaps being filled with reclaimed items that tell a story. In the kitchen, wall lights salvaged from a ship provide an industrial edge, with a 1920s cast-iron sink found by Lyndsay nestled in a contemporary custom-stone countertop. An Indian daybed the couple stumbled upon in a warehouse in Vermont, that was 'destroyed but had so much potential', is now positioned in the living room, with textiles such as the white linen curtains made by the pair hung on restored curtain rods in the main bedroom. These elements are complemented by recurring patina-rich textures: wrap-around grooved wood walls in daughter Charlotte's room, limestone tiling in the main bathroom, Pietra Cardosa (a durable soft grey stone) countertops and hard-wearing accessories such as sisal rugs and linen upholstery. Things here feel deliberately unfinished, unpretentious.

'We want our home to look and feel good,' says Lyndsay, 'but it's equally as important that the space continues to contribute to the environment while remaining functional and relevant. Our home is over a hundred years old; our aim is that the choices we make and the materials we use will still make sense 100 years from now.'

The kitchen includes a
sapele wood kitchen island,
exotic wood bar stools and
mahogany shelving designed
and built by Lyndsay and
Fitzhugh. The playful loft bed
located above the kitchen,
was designed by Lyndsay as
the first guest room in the
home. Lighting was salvaged
from an Indian ship and the
sink is a vintage 1920s piece.

The sliding door that leads to the bathroom used
to be the door to the sheep barn on the farm where
Fitzhugh grew up in New Hampshire. Fitzhugh patched
the original holes using wood in a similar tone that he
found in a skip.

The dining table was designed and made by Lyndsay and
Fitzhugh on the evening of the renovation's completion.
The wall mounted sculpture, located above the fireplace,
was made by Fitzhugh from repurposed wood scraps.

Describe your style in three words.
Light. Tactile. Ordered.

What does sustainability mean to you?
Reusing and maintaining things from the past.

What are your top four tips for creating a reimagined home?
> Always try to choose the hand of the maker over the machine.

> Opt for natural and durable materials that will preserve your space for years to come.

> Work with the bones of the building you have, not the one you wish you had, and let the property's heritage inform the design.

> When you fall in love with an item and it doesn't make sense, buy it anyway. This could be when you're 14 or 80 but when you finally locate the property to bring it all together, you will find yourself surrounded by pieces you love, and your space will be transformed into a home.

Who or what are your inspirations in terms of sustainable design?
I've always been inspired by my grandparents and the way their generation was raised to reuse and appreciate what they own and fix what's broken.

What triggers your creativity?
Each other. Whether it's over dinner, lying in bed or making breakfast, the creative conversation is ongoing; ideas are always being shared and built upon.

Your home makes you feel . . .
Replenished. Restored.

What interior item couldn't you live without?
Our storage units. A calm space has a major influence on our emotional well-being, and on how we navigate the space.

Paint colour of choice?
Super White by Benjamin Moore. It is the perfect foil for letting materials and textures shine through.

Tell me something nobody knows about your home.
It will never be finished. We will always want to add another piece of furniture or artwork. It is the epitome of slow decorating.

Finish the sentence: a considered home should be . . .
A detailed reflection of the people who live there.

The playful penthouse reviving 1960s materials

'Jelly souffle, prawn cocktail and ornate Tupperware,' says Monique Woodward, creative director of interiors and architectural brand WOWOWA , of her starting point for the 1960s-style modern penthouse, dubbed Modo Pento, that she designed for a client in St Kilda, Melbourne. An unusual mood board for a renovation, but one that allowed Woodward to create a smorgasbord of texture, colour and shape in keeping with the 'out of the ordinary' ethos that has come to define her brand.

Woodward co-founded WOWOWA with her husband Scott in 2010, at the age of 24, with the aim of melding exuberant design with sustainable principles. The company has since evolved into an award-winning B-Corp-certified architectural practice. 'For us, caring for country, regeneration and storytelling are always our starting points,' says Woodward. 'Our first move is to articulate how we can repair and honour the land our project sits within and be good story listeners for our clients.' As such, WOWOWA schemes cannot be defined as a particular style: they are considered yet non-prescriptive; sustainably led while bursting with character and *joie de vivre*.

Modo is situated at the top of a three-storey brown-brick complex, last renovated in the early 2000s to include the addition of a second living space, bar room and wrap-around patio area on the existing rooftop. Rooms, although compact, are split over several levels, which gives a sense of spaciousness despite an abundance of awkward corners. The client brief for Woodward was to sensitively return the apartment to its original condition while amplifying the design of the era.

'It was very 1990s,' she says about the new-build layout and stud walls put in place by the previous owners. Every wall was painted white, with chrome fittings and laminate surfaces peppered throughout. Rooms felt disjointed and the style wasn't in keeping with the essential character of the building. Instead of having a demolition plan, however, Woodward hatched a reuse plan, focused on embellishing the existing bones of the building. The original parquet floors were repatched, the chimney was re-clad in fluted tiles, the sliding glass doors spruced up with a lick of paint, old tiles repurposed as a surrounding wall in the new BBQ area and ceilings re-lined with Victorian ash timber for further insulation. 'Renovations are not about what you take out of a space, but what you leave in,' she says.

This philosophy extends to weaving in the history of the surrounding area. 'St Kilda is adorned with glamourous homes and apartment buildings,' says Woodward. In the early 20th century, the streets were lined with stately mansions, which then became empty rooms to be filled by the *émigré* crowd of musicians and artists after the war. A European-infused culture of late-night cafes and jazz ensued, creating an atmosphere of laid-back vibrancy that led to an influx of modernist apartment blocks. Modo is the embodiment of this time: turquoise imbued walls and colour-block joinery that evoke the nostalgic charm of the 1950s, punctuated with hand-crafted mid-century furniture and bright mosaics that encapsulate the optimism of a post-war Melbourne. Curved furniture and fluted surfaces echo the fluid shapes of Woodward's dessert-inspired mood board, while making a playful reference to the age of the 'domestic goddess' when convenience cookware dominated kitchens – the irony being 'convenience' was meant to afford working women more time. 'I wanted a scheme that was yummy to the eye, but also told a story,' she explains.

It's important not to mistake Modo's joyful schemes for a lack of seriousness, however. Despite Woodward having a dislike for 'boring' spaces, she is equally passionate about the brand's commitment to sustainability and regenerative design. 'I'm kind of a camouflaged radical environmentalist,' she affirms. 'I want our renovations to produce rather than consume energy.'

Modo is a solid mid-century modern block made from thick brick walls that gives 'excellent thermal mass', underpinned with concrete slabs that separate the floors and provide further temperature regulation. Woodward added double glazing to the existing timber frames, along with a new hydro heating system and combi-boiler (a high-efficiency water heater and boiler in a single compact unit) which requires less energy and is cheaper to run.

Paints, despite their punchy shades, are low-VOC for healthier air quality – 'if you're choosing a sustainable paint, you can still choose one that happens to be a fun colour' – with low-energy LED lights incorporated throughout and solar panels installed on the roof. On the patio, an awning from Facebook Marketplace sits alongside new pebbled decking that has been sealed with specks of recycled plastic and the original breeze block guardrail. Furniture throughout is either repurposed or sourced locally.

Despite Modo being a penthouse positioned in 'the sky', there is also a strong connection to the land: Australian-crafted timbers in the form of custom-built joinery throughout, solid spotted gum kitchen benchtops, ironbark and blackwood veneers and blond herringbone flooring that connects the kitchen, living and library space, all culminating in a celebration of natural materials. Even playful design moments, such as the collection of decorative ceramic kangaroos that form a vignette on a joinery ledge, indicate an historical connection to the surrounding landscape. 'I don't believe in ornaments for ornaments' sake,' explains Woodward. 'Items have to work hard, to convey a story.'

Spaces, although highly decorative, earn their keep within the design scheme. 'We aim to design "forever homes" for clients; rooms must have a double if not triple function,' says Woodward, who actively resists working with clients who do not intend to live in their new homes for at least five years, to reduce waste within the housing market. Rooms, just like the materials featured within them, are built with longevity in mind. The kitchen, for example, is an Aladdin's cave of storage options, with wall-mounted cabinets made of locally sourced ash, integrated appliances to free up counter space and a concealed wine rack located above the cabinets to utilize every inch.

As such, a WOWOWA home accommodates and reflects the lives of its occupants as they evolve, without veering into the mundane. Here sustainability goes beyond sourcing natural materials and shopping local. It is joyous, vibrant and daring.

A modernist dream.

The patio overlooking St Kilda is a favourite space with its colourful pebbled decking sealed with recycled plastic, a candy-striped awning from Facebook Marketplace and new built-in barbecue area formed using old tiles repurposed as the surrounding wall.

Monique Woodward

The kitchen features a modern take on a 1950s interior with colour block kitchen joinery, mottled glazed ceramic finger tiles and playful teal grout. The kitchen benchtops are made from spotted gum, an Australian hardwood timber known for its durability, with ironbark and blackwood veneers.

Decorative items and artwork featured throughout the home has been collected over the years, including a set of vintage ship trays, a "Tuscan Landscape" watercolour, painted by a friend of the family, and a ceramic vase with houses etched on it that was given to the homeowner as a gift. The large wooden artwork is by UK based artist, Sara Willett, and depicts thousands of concentric circles carved onto multiple layers of paint.

A custom-made upholstered headboard in Yale Blue compliments the peacock carpeting and creates a plush cocoon with bespoke built-in side tables and timber joinery to tie in with the apartment's natural materials. A luxurious lilac velvet curtain 'doorway' creates a tactile wing-within-a-wing effect.

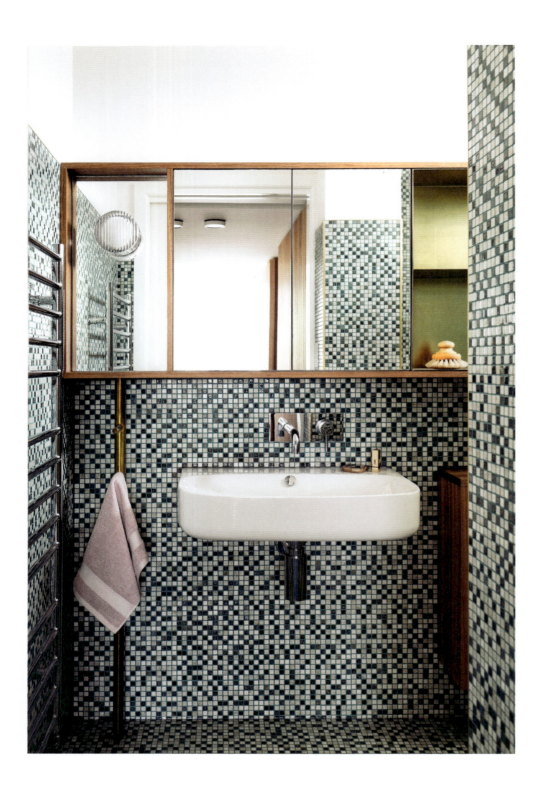

The en-suite bathroom features a wall-mounted sink, utilitarian cabinets, timber joinery, brass flourishes and vibrant mosaic tiles that each echo the penthouse's mid-century history.

Describe your style in three words.
Colourful. Narrative. Considered.

What does sustainability mean to you?
Circularity and regenerative design – they are more interesting than simply maintaining the status quo of current sustainability targets.

What are your top four tips for creating a reimagined home?
> Design thinking: hire an architect to help you execute your vision with the highest quality materials. It may be costly in the short term, but the long-term results will be worth it.

> Specify handmade materials for your renovation. They are of a higher quality and will last longer.

> Shop from your region or as locally as possible.

> Personalize your space by embedding delightful stories that reflect the heritage of your property and that mean something to you.

Who or what are your inspirations in terms of sustainable design?
Australia's First Nations People are our biggest inspirations. For 60,000 years they cared for these lands. We should celebrate their knowledge to best understand how to design in a sustainable and regenerative way for future generations.

What triggers your creativity?
The past: reminiscing about the walks I took with my grandfather when I was a child. He was so innovative and we would create all sorts of magical worlds together. I think I get my creativity from him, with the more practical side from my grandmother.

Your home makes you feel . . .
Like the best version of you, surrounded with stories and moments that make you smile.

What interior item couldn't you live without?
Artwork to adorn the walls. My favourite thing to do with clients is go to galleries and select precious works to complement the spaces we design.

Paint colour of choice?
Anything earthy.

Tell me something nobody knows about this home.
It belongs to a famous political person.

Finish the sentence: a considered home should be . . .
Planned well – a home is nothing without a good plan.

A Victorian terrace transformed
into a thriving ecosystem

The expression that you shouldn't judge a book by its cover might also apply to houses. Specifically, this house. Because while the unassuming Victorian facade of serial tech entrepreneur Puli Liyanagama's property in Peckham, which he shares with his partner Jessica and rescue cats Croutons and Queen, implies that it is stereotypically suburban, this is a home that is anything but.

Liyanagama's home is less about interior status symbols and more about how it promotes emotional and physical well-being. 'I wanted to live in a place that reflected my background and culture,' he says of his Sri Lankan heritage.

Liyanagama grew up next to Number 11 House, the iconic Colombo residence of the pioneer of tropical modernism in Sri Lanka, Geoffrey Bawa, and became inspired by Bawa's fusion of modernist design sensibilities with the natural elements. Liyanagama was particularly drawn to the vernacular of Bawa's Kandalama (an eco-friendly hotel engulfed by nature) and the way it appears to meld into the surrounding landscape. 'I like to think that Bawa's intention was for the design of the hotel to be ever-evolving, only fully complete when overrun with vegetation,' he says. This poetic notion forms the backbone of his own space: a modernist interpretation of *Sleeping Beauty*, where nature informs the language of the architecture rather than the other way around.

Liyanagama enlisted the design acumen of South African-born architect Neil Dusheiko to help carry out his vision for the space. 'It was a classic Victorian house built in the 1890s,' says Liyanagama of the original three bedrooms and compartmentalized living areas laid out in the usual fashion. The previous owners had occupied it since the 1960s and left it relatively untouched in terms of structural changes. Being from similar cultures, Liyanagama and Dusheiko almost approached the existing design as 'foreigners', viewing the remaining design elements not only as novelties, but as treasured objects that needed to be preserved.

Original features are thus retained and celebrated throughout: fireplaces, stairs, balustrades and plaster mouldings; flooring a mixture of restored original boards combined with FSC-certified wood by Dinesen. 'Victorian houses are incredibly adaptable,' says Dusheiko. 'It is possible for traces of the past and glimpses of the future to coexist within the same space.'

The home was opened up through the addition of a double-height extension to the rear of the property, which increased the square footage of the kitchen area by a surprisingly modest 1.5 metres. 'Our goal was to create volume rather than expand the footprint or create additional rooms,' says Dusheiko, referring to the loss of the third bedroom in order to make space for a dressing room area and cork-tiled workspace.

A two-storey void now connects the existing portion of the home to the rear extension, putting the emphasis on the vertical to give the interiors a sense of scale and to encourage light to flow freely. Large skylights and double-glazed windows have been incorporated throughout to utilize solar energy and reduce the reliance on artificial light, in addition to enabling Liyanagama to vent the house on very hot days. Dusheiko also employed a 'stack ventilation' system whereby a vertical pipe runs through the roof to the outside of the house to regulate air pressure. 'It meant that there was less of a need to insulate many of the internal walls, allowing the original exposed brickwork to remain intact,' he says.

The project, dubbed 'House of the Elements' by Dusheiko due to the abundance of plants and natural materials – wood, stone, cork, linen – paired with large swathes of glass and charred timber cladding, is a true celebration of nature. 'I wanted to create a home that not only revels in the elements of earth, fire, water and air, but is also balanced by them,' he says. A design manifesto that culminates in the linchpin of the space: the carbon-neutral living wall.

Powered by solar energy and supplemented with harvested rainwater from a tank in the basement, the wall is a thriving ecosystem that has become home not only to a towering collection of peace lilies, calatheas, pothos and other plants native to Sri Lanka, but different types of insects that live off the plants – as well as off each other. 'It's indicative of the cycle of life,' explains Liyanagama, who sporadically releases further insects into the roaming leaves, with sun-loving species placed closer to the light and those requiring more shade towards the bottom. 'We wanted this to be a space where the house itself appears to grow and come "alive",' says Dusheiko of the wall, which continues to evolve the space organically without Liyanagama needing to maintain it. 'One day they might even take over the whole house, Bawa-style,' smiles Liyanagama, in reference to the stray tendrils already weaving themselves into the main space.

Indeed, the home possesses a seemingly boundless quality where every room, landing, floating balcony and window merges into an expanding naturescape. 'Each angle of the home was designed to look out either onto the garden or the living wall,' explains Dusheiko. 'I wanted nature to be the magnet towards which everything else in the house is pulled.'

The opposing forces of light and dark are incorporated throughout. In the kitchen, walls are swathed in a tactile charcoal resin made from crushed castor beans, with inky tones repeated in the bedrooms to enable the greenery to 'emerge' from the darkness. In contrast, the living room is a calm expanse of white, punctuated by Liyanagama's collection of books, travel mementos and houseplants that help 'purify the air', including English ivy, a weeping fig (which Liyanagama refers to as 'Morgan Treeman'), money plants, pothos and a large Bird of Paradise, affectionately named 'Leafy Gaga'.

Liyanagama's choice of furniture echoes the pared-back nature of the space – 'I use a bunch of apps to give away things' – and includes items chosen for their ability to enhance the sensorial aspects of the space, rather than distract from them. In the kitchen, a glass dining table balanced on wooden trestles only becomes fully visible when in use. 'Many would have opted for a wooden dining table in here as it's more aesthetically pleasing, but I wanted something that merged with the surroundings.' In the minimally designed bedrooms, bespoke beds are handmade using the same timber as the floor and positioned lower than the standard height to increase the sense of space. A towering three-dimensional plaster artwork by Italian artist SODA is incorporated above one of the retained fireplaces. 'You only fully notice it when the light hits it,' says Liyanagama. 'The crisp structure works in contrast to the fluid forms of the green wall.'

The overarching holistic nature of the design has not impeded Liyanagama's ability to incorporate hidden surprises throughout. The built-in bathroom, bedroom and landing cabinets open to reveal a dopamine-inducing fluorescent yellow interior, with an electric-orange metal door in the shape of a lightning bolt leading into the guest bedroom. In the downstairs bathroom, a QR code links to the history of the coconut on Wikipedia. 'My dad worked as a botanist for the Coconut Research Institute in Sri Lanka, so I had to hide a few coconuts in there somewhere,' Liyanagama says. Despite his experience in the tech world (two of his businesses have been sold to King, the makers of Candy Crush, and more recently to Apple), the QR code is the only piece of tech allowed in the house – and that includes a TV. 'Software dates quickly and goes against the founding principles of the design,' he says. 'I spend my day being "plugged in", I want my home to be somewhere I can disconnect from the pressures of modern life. To be naturally joyous.'

One of the home's statement features is the series of fractured geometric planes by Italian artist SODA that ascends through the new three-storey void crafting an interplay of light and shadow, and that changes by the hour.

The house is full of zingy surprises, including inbuilt fluoro yellow cupboard interiors featured in the guest bedroom that creates a fun interplay with the tonal plaster walls.

Initially constructed in the late 19th century, the house maintains its traditional front reception room filled with Liyanagama's collection of houseplants that help purify the air, including a weeping fig, referred to as 'Morgan Treeman', and a large Bird of Paradise named 'Leafy Gaga.' Chunky Bakelite light switches lean into the anti-tech ethos of the home and provide sensory touch points throughout.

The teak bathtub appears to sink into the floor due to the clever positioning of an expansive window frame that showcases views of the vibrant living wall. The walls are coated in polished plaster made from natural biopolymers extracted from castor beans.

Full width glazing makes a star of the spa-like garden designed by Sheila Jack, that further forges a seamless link between inside and out. A bespoke timber walkway leads to a raised brick terrace, concrete bench and corten steel reflective tank that collects rainwater. A green carpet of interplanted Soleirolia soleirolii was used as a more sustainable lawn alternative. It will continue to grow naturally without the need for intervention.

Describe your style in three words.
Minimalist. Functional. Organic.

What does sustainability mean to you?
To work with rather than against nature. My great-grandfather's house, for example, had a jackfruit tree in the middle of the living room because he refused to move it. The furniture was centred around it. This philosophy is often reflected in Sri Lankan architecture. It enables the occupant to live 'lightly', as they're not consuming too many resources to sustain themselves.

What are your top four tips for creating a reimagined home?

> Embrace minimalism and declutter where possible. Simplifying your space will enhance mental clarity and peace.

> Incorporate nature throughout with plants, natural light and materials that will create a soothing environment.

> Create personal sanctuaries by designating areas for relaxation and activities that bring joy.

> Prioritize comfort and functionality in ways that support your daily activities and lifestyle.

Who or what are your inspirations in terms of sustainable design?
It sounds obvious but Geoffrey Bawa has been a major story in my life. I've stayed in all the hotels he has designed and his own estate, Lunuganga, in Sri Lanka. His sustainably led design is an endless source of inspiration to me.

What triggers your creativity?
Being connected to the environment in some way. I often work either outside or by the living wall in the kitchen. Somewhere I can disconnect from the modern world.

Your home makes you feel . . .
Rejuvenated.

What interior item couldn't you live without?
My bookshelf. Books and plants are the only things that I keep adding to the house.

Paint colour of choice?
I tend to like stereotypical 'boring' colours: off-whites, creams, charcoal-tones that allow the surrounding elements to sing.

Tell me something nobody knows about your home.
It features so few doors that a sprinkler system had to be installed to meet fire regulations.

Finish the sentence: a considered home should be . . .
A place to rest and recharge.

The idea of reusing, rethinking and reinventing the home is nothing new – it's how many of us have decorated for years – but it is more important now than ever before. As environmental awareness grows along with financial pressures, repairability continues to become an integral part of product life cycles within the home, with people increasingly looking to fix broken or tired items rather than buying new ones.

This is a fundamental step in the circular economy, helping to limit our impact on the environment by keeping in use and circulation items that would otherwise go to landfill.

The resurgence of heritage craft techniques such as *Passementerie* (the art of creating decorative trimmings such as tassels, braids and gold and silver cord) marquetry and chair weaving has resulted in the handcrafted becoming highly regarded as art forms within the home. Whilst historical mending techniques such as *kintsugi*, the Japanese method of repairing broken ceramics and porcelains, celebrate the wear and tear of an items past life to create a unique home, filled with pieces rich in context, history and diversity.

For many, reinventing can be as simple and cost-effective as buying a second-hand lamp base and adding an existing shade, repainting an old chair instead of replacing it, or adding a mural to your wardrobe or cupboard door as a reimagined piece of artwork. In the London home of a textile designer, bungee cord has been repurposed as a simple yet statement stair guard. In the Amsterdam home of a photographer and stylist, the majority of items, including a chandelier made from ceramic spoons, have been remade using items rescued from skips.

The result is a collection of homes that are bespoke to the owners, full of considered items to be treasured and passed down to future generations.

Reuse, Rethink, Reinvent

Historic techniques create
a timeless townhouse

Founder and director of sustainable lifestyle brand, Resinn, Kate Blower, describes the style of her four-storey renovation project – shared with husband Erik Öhrström, and their two children as a 'mash-up of English and Scandinavian design meets heritage'. Dramatic florals are paired with exposed pipework, lime plaster walls and weathered materials, with every element coexisting to create a family home and business that is both considered and adventurous in equal measure.

The transformation from typical Victorian townhouse to a home that celebrates the magical interplay between historic architecture and contemporary flourishes happens the moment you step through the front door into a vestibule clad in grasscloth and original architraves and cornices – originally buried under layers of paint 'thicker than wedding cake icing' – lead you on a sensory journey up the staircase to the first floor, where a reading nook, 'snug' area, kitchen and main bedroom kitted out in handmade and reclaimed finds await. The children's bedrooms are located on the third floor, with the basement housing a boot room, WC, bathroom, kitchenette and the environmentally conscious lifestyle store and monthly pop-up restaurant run by the couple, Resinn. The 'heartbeat' of the house, Resinn is the manifestation of the couple's design philosophy: narrative, timeless and considered.

The name stands for 'everything that resonates with us', explains Blower of the space that sells plants and flowers, locally roasted coffee and handmade interior accessories. Originally the kitchen of the house during the 1870s, the large exposed-brick chimney area was where they stored barrels of coal, with the servants' living quarters located in the front. Original features remain intact and the space is now decorated with classic black wooden chairs, wrought iron marble-topped tables and exposed copper pipes repurposed as storage rails and makeshift taps. 'It's cheaper and better for the environment than buying off the shelf,' says Blower of the naturally distressed aesthetic that feels a touch more Copenhagen than Sunderland.

When the property first came on the market, the couple were renting a flat 20 minutes down the road, with Blower working two jobs to save for a mortgage. It was originally used as student accommodation, but the owner wanted it converted back into a family home. Despite the house not being family ready – there was a gaping hole in the roof, floors covered in mangy carpet, which was 'more cloth than carpet', and severe water damage throughout – Blower fell in love with the creative potential, scale, proportions and original features. 'It had sash windows, wooden floorboards, ornate cornicing and exposed brickwork, but it needed a lot of work,' she says.

The budget was super tight for a renovation project on this scale, with the couple earmarking £7,000 for the structural costs, which were soon sunk into making the kitchen and bathroom 'habitable'. This left them little financial wiggle room to tackle the upstairs, which was clad in woodchip paper – 'an absolute nightmare in an old property as it makes everything sweat and crumble' – and several stud walls that needed to be removed to restore the space to its original layout and prevent it becoming compartmentalized. They needed a solution that returned the house to its heritage glory and also saved them money in the long term.

Blower went down a wormhole on YouTube and found videos by historic building conservationist Peter Ward (founder of Heritage House), who talked her through how to rectify the renovations often done to old properties that stop them from breathing. 'He explained every single material that should be used in a Victorian building and how important it is for the health of your home to take the space back to these materials,' she says.

Using Ward's tutorials as a guide, Blower taught herself how to apply breathable lime plaster to the walls, a traditional type of mortar that helps absorb carbon monoxide from the air and prevent condensation. Blower mixed it with distemper paint, a powdered chalk mixture that is watered down to create a rippling effect across the walls. 'I wanted to see all of the natural imperfections and inflections,' she says.

To insulate a home of this scale without breaking the bank, Blower installed linseed oil putty on the windows. 'It's made with horsehair that you slot in between the frame before filling it with lime-based mortar to prevent drafts naturally,' she explains. The majority of the windows are single glazed, with Blower adding a beaded trim (another YouTube tutorial gem) that goes around the window and has a little brush on the back to prevent drafts from coming in. Following a conversation with a tradesman who told her to rip the original windows out and square them off with plastic uPVC, Blower also restored the original timber window frames (using tools including a router from Lidl) to make a slightly deeper bed for thicker glass. 'It's much better for the environment and saved us a fortune,' she says. 'All of the materials you need are readily available, easy to use and healthier for the planet. We're just not informed about them in the same way as quick-fix materials such as cement and PVC.'

Any original elements of the house that were damaged, such as the internal doors – of which there was only one left intact – have been lovingly restored in the vein of the original design. 'We tracked down a glass manufacturer that specialized in glass dating back to the 1920s and asked them to replicate the design,' says Blower, who also replaced all of the modern hardware added when the space was a student accommodation with reclaimed alternatives. 'Everything feeds back into the building's history.'

To that end, most of the furnishings are either reclaimed, inherited or handmade and come with a story. 'I invest in future heirlooms,' says Blower. 'Things that you're going to treasure for the rest of your life and can be handed down to future generations.' Design inspiration ranges from Facebook Marketplace to Etsy, eBay and reclamation yards, with Blower frequently trawling auction catalogues before they go live in the hunt for one-of-a-kind pieces.

Each find is the decor equivalent of a statement necklace, elevating shelves, nooks and drawers into moments of simple artistry. Blower's hero items include the sink in the first-floor WC, which had been ripped out of the Bridge Hotel in Newcastle and was found on Facebook Marketplace for £40 – 'it has a few hairline cracks in it but that only adds to the natural patina' – the ceramic pig she found at a reclamation yard that takes pride of place on the kitchen dresser and is a nod to the butcher's that Blower's family ran for decades, and the fold-down seats in the adjoining boot room that originally hailed from a Victorian train station.

Alongside hunting for reclaimed pieces and innovative DIY, Blower's passion is colour and how it can orchestrate a mood. 'The Victorians married colour with the natural light and scale of the space to optimize the enjoyment in each room,' she says about her choice of an oilslick palette by family-run heritage brand Warner House that ranges from squid-ink through to chocolate and ochre and reflects the history of the building. Textiles within a similar colour palette reside throughout in either a shade lighter or darker than the surrounding walls. 'We call it cake on cake,' says Blower of the 'chocolate box' main bedroom where a handmade canopy of rich brown velvet (the offcuts of which were used to make the surrounding lampshades) cascades down a mushroom-hued FSC-certified patterned wallpaper and merges into soft brown linen sheets. It's a pile-on of warmth.

Blower is drawn to the comfort of 'things' – objects, patterns and textures. It's a fascination that stems from her education in costume design and experience of retail design for high-street giants such as Urban Outfitters in London and H&M in Sweden for more than fifteen years. The pace of the house is informed by her intrinsic sense of materiality: from the heavy velvet curtains in the boot room, edged with frills and fringe aplenty (made by Blower), to layered linens in the first-floor snug area and a cotton canopy in her daughter's room, hung from repurposed wardrobe rails. More playful elements – the bold House of Hackney floral wallpaper in the living room and plywood cabin bed in her son's room, handmade by Blower in the style of a ship's sleeping quarters and coated in chalk paint – prevent the aesthetic from veering into 'trad' while still providing a connection to the past.

In that sense, the home has a déjà vu quality. The materials, items and traditional techniques used all tell stories of past lives while being reincarnated to create something new, exciting and ever evolving. 'For me, this is more than a house,' says Blower. 'It's more than a home even. It's a place where the pull of the past and hope for the future go full circle.'

142

The daybed located on the first floor landing was a second-hand auction find that Blower made the tufted mattress and cushions for using reproduced 1870s fabric from heritage brand Warner House. The space was originally a make-shift shower room and storage area before being transformed into a landing space. The walls are bathed in breathable lime plaster mixed with distemper paint.

144

The splashback is made from ceramic tiles Blower found on eBay that are also repeated in the landing WC and basement bathroom. The storage rails are repurposed copper pipes and brackets, with the shelf above made from pine that Blower scorched using an ancient Japanese method of wood preservation, called Shou Sugi Ban, whereby planks of wood are charred to preserve and strengthen them.

The original cornicing was previously buried under thick layers of paint that Blower sanded down. They form part of the vestibule area, which is clad in grasscloth, and original wooden staircase framed by a fretwork arch.

Kate Blower

The ceramic sink in the utility room was an auction find, with the
unit made from old bricks that were being discarded by a neighbour,
rendered in lime plaster by Blower. Blower made the velvet curtain
in the upstairs boot room as a tactile door replacement using
reproduced 1870s fabric from Warner House.

The bed in her son's room was inspired by old European cabin beds designed to keep out droughts during winter before the existence of central heating. Blower built a timber pine frame that she cladded in plywood and painted using chalk paint before sealing with clear wax.

Describe your style in three words.
Story-driven. Heritage. Playful.

What does sustainability mean to you?
Taking what already exists and evolving it.

What are your top four tips for creating a reimagined home?
> Try to use second-hand as much as possible. Fifty per cent of a room should be sourced from places that have a history and provide context.

> Incorporate often-overlooked humble materials to future-proof your space. Linseed oil, for example, will live for 150 years in your home, helping to prevent leaks and drafts.

> Don't rush the decorative process. Live in the space for a while and think about what it is going to be used for and how you want to enjoy it. Then start small, finding inspiration in a paint colour or piece of furniture to get the creative cogs whirring.

> Surround yourself with like-minded people who are on a similar journey and share similar design sensibilities. Help and encourage each other along the way.

Who or what are your inspirations in terms of sustainable design?
The work of sculptor and installation artist Antony Gormley. He illustrates how nature, human beings and the cosmos are all interconnected.

What triggers your creativity?
I'm drawn to the coastline – the shapes and formations that I see on my walks. I love coming across things that the sea has naturally sculpted and thrown back out onto the beach after years of being tossed around in the ocean. I collect all sorts.

Your home makes you feel . . .
Creative. Restored. Secure.

What interior item couldn't you live without?
It has to be the little loos that we have now. I call them the 'panic rooms'. I'll go in there and hide if I just need a minute to reflect.

Paint colour of choice?
Glowing Amber by heritage brand Warner House in our boot room. It's like a dirty mustard that glows when the light hits it and makes you feel like you've been wrapped up in a blanket with a cup of tea.

Tell me something nobody knows about your home.
We have a 'Room of Gloom' that has been locked for two years and counting. We can't face going in there!

Finish the sentence: a considered home should be . . .
A space that serves you on a practical level while filling you with moments of daily joy.

Reclaimed rarities turn 19th-century
flats into a versatile home

Allowing the existing house to inform the refurb rather than the other way round is an unusual approach for an interior designer to take, but one that fits perfectly with the design ethos of Maria Speake, co-founder of renowned salvage brand Retrouvius. For Speake, design revolves around one word – respect. 'Respect for what has gone before us – the hard-won items and bones of that space – and how to honour and reuse them, rather than replace,' says Speake of the philosophy that has placed Retrouvius at the forefront of sustainable design for the past thirty years and counting.

Retrouvius was co-founded by Speake and her husband, Adam Hills, in 1993 (with Speake spearheading the design side of the business, Hills the salvage side) as an antidote to fast design, after working on an architectural project together at university that found them rifling through discarded building materials in a skip. It was an experience that sparked their love and passion for conservation, which soon grew to encompass the sourcing of salvaged 'oddments' and rarities such as reclaimed stone, tropical hardwoods, statement one-offs, lighting and textiles. 'If it was being thrown out, we'd have it,' smiles Speake, who utilized such 'oddities' to create homes focused on the well-made, precious and considered.

This is reflected in a 19th-century house in Hampstead designed by Speake and the Retrouvius team. 'It was previously a rabbit warren of bedsits,' recalls Speake of the space, whose Herculean challenge it was to convert it into one cohesive family home for an American couple, Jenny and Marcus, and their three children, aged between nine and 16. The refashioned space now consists of five storeys, including an entrance lobby, L-shaped kitchen dining room, basement and attic.

'It's a sprawling space,' says Speake – one which could easily have become a visually intimidating, gallery-esque house filled with pieces to make visitors 'oooh' and 'ah' every time they turned a corner. But, despite initial appearances and the preconceived notions of bougie eateries and 'latte art' one might have of Hampstead, the space is less showy and more nuanced, with materials and pieces chosen for longevity, durability and their ability to be adapted along the way.

The attic, previously consisting of two separate rooms, is a case in point. 'As the attic roof was pitched, we could move and cut the existing staircase down to create space for a new landing area,' explains Speake. This addition allowed the eldest son, who was studying for his A-levels at the time, to have his own area in the house. 'I wanted it to be a space that would not only cater for his needs now, but also the family's needs in the future,' describes Speake, who envisioned a magical world for the younger children to grow into, and for future grandchildren to explore.

To that end, the space is clad in vibrant, reclaimed tongue-and-groove panelling, with the existing playful porthole window left to overlook London and spark the imagination of young minds. Ample storage options have also been built in or concealed behind the boards, as well as under beds, to allow for future alterations. 'If the family gets fed up with the colour or it starts to feel dated, they can easily paint over it while still retaining the practicality and underlying quality of the material,' says Speake of the tongue-and-groove. A philosophy that can be applied to the whole house.

Unlike many central London refurbs, the original 'fabric' of the building has remained untouched; original masonry and Victorian timber-braced brickwork left exposed ('it would have been outrageous to conceal it with plaster') along with limed floorboards, plaster cornices and the backbone of the house – the spiral wooden staircase, once concealed when the property was a series of bedsits but now a celebration of the new-found volume and scale. Even leftover floorboards have been repurposed, with some used to hide the cistern on the first-floor bathroom wall, others as boxing. Where it was not possible to salvage existing elements, Speake has replicated the additions in the same vein as the original design. The double doors with leaded-glass panels that feature in the first-floor hallway were made to match the original lobby doors. 'We wanted the house to feel like it had always been there,' she says of the 'slavish pastiche approach'.

Nothing here is fussy or ornamental, however, with Speake preferring unapologetically robust materials that pack a creative punch. In the main bedroom, an oversized headboard is made using hand-dyed velvet offcuts from the bedroom curtains, with the adjoining en-suite bathroom accessed through Dutch etched-glass doors that lead to a wall lined with sliding wardrobes created from salvaged art deco glass panels, linen upholstery and repurposed old oak drawers. 'I like materials that show the wrinkles and kinks of time,' she says.

The utility room walls, clad in cheese boards (previously used for storing maturing gouda in the Netherlands and still displaying original markings), are a further example. 'Their chunky dimensions lend themselves to joinery,' says Speake, who makes it her mission not to cut up or into salvaged pieces where possible, preferring instead to plan around the dimensions of the existing item rather than the other way round. The rest of the utility room boasts a reclaimed sink, sourced by Hills, surrounded by a Vitralite glass splashback (a hard-wearing pigmented glass popular in the 1920s and 1930s that is stain-resistant and impervious to moisture). It is a look that is driven not by perfection, but by function and the joy of materiality.

In the guest bathroom, a backdrop slab of blue marble, rescued by Hills from a local stonemason who was downsizing, has been refashioned as an eye-catching yet practical shower backdrop. Likewise in the ground-floor WC, where an unusual salvaged red ceramic sink and brackets sourced from salvo.co.uk complement the mottled tomato swirl of the bathroom door – an original piece sanded by Speake to reveal layers of old paint.

One of the stand-out spaces in the property, however, and one that has subsequently become a firm favourite among the Pinterest tribe, is the zingy blue and green bathroom and adjoining dressing room. The salvaged Crittall doors were sourced by Hills from the London School of Economics and set the direction of the sea-tone palette repeated in the attic and en-suite bathroom. As with all items sourced by Hills or Speake, the doors came to the property like this. Nothing has been repainted or tweaked to fit a certain aesthetic or 'trend'. The bath surround is made from reclaimed Iroko worktops (a hardwood saved from municipal buildings such as school science laboratories) and framed with 'fake Iznik' tiles – 'fake' as the only real ones adorn the Topkapi palace in Istanbul – from Emery & Cie that bring an informed historical narrative to the design.

This is a resounding thread throughout: Speake's aesthetic interweaves many design periods, styles and moments without veering into cliché. Here, a 'mix and match' approach that spans genres has been employed, with many pieces, such as the dining table and fish artwork (a kids' school project) being the homeowner's own. Speake sourced the 1940s dining chairs, re-covered in gelato-coloured corduroy, along with the vintage Dutch glass pendant lights from Belgian antiques dealer 2oeme Siècle. In the kitchen, where the addition of a contemporary SubZero fridge was a deal-breaker for the owner, Speake added a contrasting pair of vintage Dutch design armchairs – also upholstered in corduroy – and Scandi-style upholstered bar stools for a 'lived-in' vibe. In the living room, a framed quilt made using scraps of silk the owner inherited from her great-grandmother takes pride of place above their existing Caravane sofa, with Speake sourcing complementing elements such as a 1950s Italian ceiling light. 'Reusing doesn't always mean going "looking" for green credentials,' explains Speake. 'Sometimes it's about the sense of history you get when you utilize an item that has a past life, a story.'

Despite the high ceilings of the house, Speake has woven in playful details that belie the grandness of the space. In the kitchen, a generous floor-to-ceiling checked curtain in shades of mustard and tomato, sourced from Dutch supplier De Ploeg, is used as a tactile and fun room divider. Elsewhere, a former surveyor's measure has been repurposed as a novel stair rail. 'I wanted to create a new home while celebrating the old,' says Speake, who has offered to revisit the space when the owners fancy a change.

The need has yet to arise.

The downstairs WC features a reclaimed sink and brackets.
The wallpaper is a map of the surrounding Hampstead area.

In the utility room, a reclaimed sink is framed by a vibrant green Vitralite glass splashback impervious to water damage and stains. Storage cabinets are made from Iroko wood. The walls are clad in chunky cheese boards previously used for storing maturing gouda.

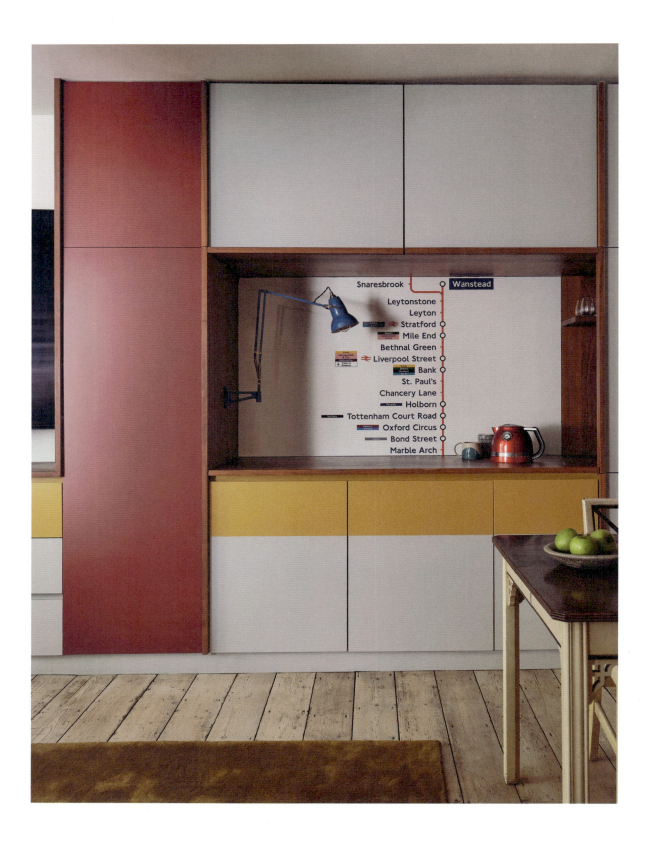

The ground floor comprises a guest bedroom and bathroom, fitness pool and teenage relaxation zone with a designated coffee and tea area defined by an original enamelled London tube map backdrop. On the wall of the ground floor and between the first and second floors, the plaster was stripped off, leaving the original Victorian timber-braced brickwork exposed.

163

An eye-catching panel of 'Faux Iznik' tiles reflects the colours of the Crittall doors that lead into the room and that were salvaged from the London School of Economics. The bath has a reclaimed Iroko surround, with patina-rich brass fixtures and fittings.

Describe your style in three words.
Reused. RE-resource-FUL. Refreshing.

What does sustainability mean to you?
An approach, an attitude, a way of life.

What are your top four tips for creating a reimagined home?
> Think of it as a cycle and the environmental impact your home will have throughout that cycle.

> Start with what already exists. It will form the backbone of the design.

> Do keep things simple. Good design should be considered.

> Think of future reuse for not only your family, but the future generations to come.

Who or what are your inspirations in terms of sustainable design?
The amazing materials we come across that nobody else wants – and the yards, salvagers and network that keep salvage in circulation.

What triggers your creativity?
Seeing items others would disregard.

Your home makes you feel . . .
Recharged.

What interior item couldn't you live without?
A well-filled tea station!

Paint colour of choice?
We're less about colours and more about non-chemical and breathable wall finishes such as plaster and brick.

Tell me something nobody knows about this home.
The bricks were made from clay dug locally in Hampstead.

Finish the sentence: a considered home should be . . .
One that allows you to live how you want to live and matches the fullness of texture, soul and emotional quota of the inhabitants.

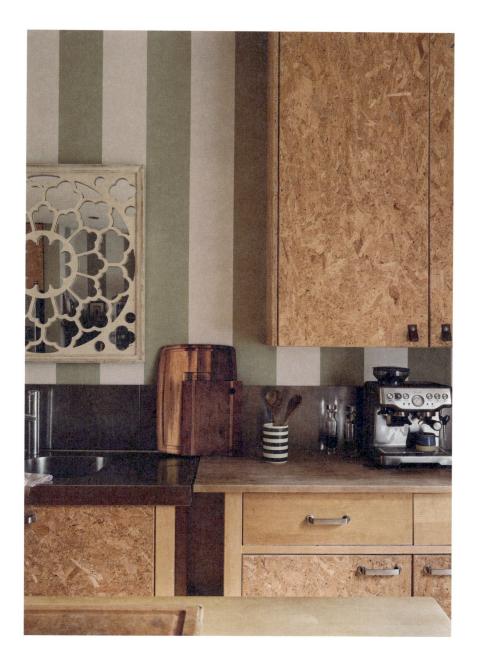

An artful Victorian terrace made
with recycled materials

I t's apt that this house, filled with creative flair and Bloomsbury-esque touches, was built at the peak of the Arts and Crafts movement. With its patterned textiles, vibrant paintwork and handmade furniture, the interiors are a joyous reflection of an era of creative exploration.

This comes as no surprise given that the homeowner is Jules Haines, founder of award winning sustainable textiles brand Haines Collection, a resale platform for designer fabrics from brands such as Christopher Farr, GP & J Baker and Pierre Frey, that would otherwise be destined for landfill. 'I grew up next to an old Singer sewing machine,' reminisces Haines. 'It was at a time when there was no social media or TV streaming channels, so I spent a lot of time sewing, cutting and sticking.' These skills are now reflected in every nook and cranny of her Victorian terrace in Tunbridge Wells, where she lives with her husband Ollie and their two children, Jemima and Edward.

As a result, there are few areas that don't feature old materials masterfully reworked into something new: lampshades made from remnants of dress fabric, drawer handles made from tired belts and curtains from a charity shop reworked as a pantry 'skirtain'. Not to mention the stair guard Haines constructed from repurposed bungee cord (fastened with brass pipe holders at the bottom), initially intended as a cost-effective temporary solution to tide her over until she could build a 'real' one. 'I was working with a restricted budget and had to find a way to stop Jemima, who was one at the time, from falling off the stairs,' she recalls. The family has since grown to love it.

For Haines, sustainability isn't just about repurposing, however. It's about focusing on renewable materials and preventing waste. 'If I fall in love with something, I always try and find it second-hand first,' she says. In the ground-floor dining room, plates amassed over the years from charity shops sit above an oak dining table made of old railway sleepers. In the pantry, salvaged scaffolding shelves, painted in the same vibrant red as the living-room shelving, house a variety of jars Haines inherited from her grandmother and collected over the years. The pendant light was 3D-printed from discarded fishing nets. Anything that she can't find new, such as the family sofa for example, becomes a 'forever' piece. 'I've had it for 15 years and will just reupholster it when the time comes,' she says.

For those who do want to buy new but are also keen to minimize their impact on the environment, Haines has created Haines Curates, a branch of the brand that only sells textiles from designers such as Pukka Print and Sophia Frances that put sustainable production first, from the transparent supply chain to the recyclable packaging. Fabrics, rugs and cushions may be brand new, but they are also repurposed, made from ethically sourced biodegradable materials, or naturally dyed with colourants derived from plants or vegetables. 'Sustainability isn't about beating yourself up if you want to buy something new for your home,' says Haines.

When the family first moved in, the space had been 'modernized', with all of the original period features stripped out and replaced with contemporary fixtures and fittings. The walls, floors and original marble fireplaces had been doused in a palette of grey and charcoal (Haines is still stripping black paint off the fireplaces) and felt stark and cold. Haines set about rein-stating dado rails and repainting the space in heritage tones of rich red, mustard and navy, which are repeated throughout and illustrate her deep-rooted respect for the period of the property. 'I'm only the custodian of the space – somebody that's moving through it for this period – but felt I had to restore it to its former glory,' she says.

Despite having had a hoard of textiles, Pinterest boards and ideas from the day she received the keys, Haines redesigned the space slowly, determined not to knock through walls or rip out any of the remaining existing features. Luckily, the space had strong architectural bones so there was no need to rush in. 'You need to live in a space to connect to it and understand how it works,' she says. Even now Haines insists that the house isn't finished. 'There's always stuff I want to do, and in a way, I don't want it to be finished. I love hunting for things, the creative process.'

Haines is not a trained designer, but her penchant for colour, texture and pattern has resulted in a deeply decorative and considered home where no two rooms look the same. In the en-suite bathroom, a contemporary shade of cobalt (dubbed 'visual caffeine' by Haines) adds depth to the small space, whereas in the guest bedroom, the walls cushions and headboard are clad in heritage florals, with a framed vintage saddlebag Haines found on eBay, repurposed as a piece of art above the bed. 'I like the juxtaposition of the contemporary with the vintage,' she muses, reflecting on her penchant for blending contrasting elements.

But while Haines may be savvy with a staple and glue gun, her creations are far from the DIY horrors we remember from the 1990s. The paint may be from tester pots, and some of the fabrics might be limited, slightly imperfect or from a 'previous season', but Haines insists that so long as you enjoy the challenge of getting stuck-in, anyone can create luxurious designs for the home on a budget.

The fireplace located in the ground floor dining room, embellished with hand-painted circles and swirls reminiscent of Charleston House, is a case in point. It was originally a gas fire with thick dark wooden shelves on either side, which Haines turned on their sides and used to frame the fireplace, before adding textured beading and painting the whole thing in the dramatic deep red of Pompadour by Edward Bulmer. 'It helped anchor the space,' she says. Another example are the sage green and white stripes in the kitchen, painted by Haines using leftover sample colours donated by a friend. 'Our cupboards are made from repurposed chipboard so we needed an element of colour to make the space more interesting.'

Haines believes that a reluctance to DIY is due not just to the stigma but an inherent anxiety people have of getting things wrong. 'I never go confidently into a project,' she says. 'The goal is not to be a perfectionist. If you chip the wooden shelf, or the paint is a bit patchy, then that is part of the story of your home. It gives your home a uniqueness.' To that end, Haines never sets out with a particular project in mind. Rather, she spends time watching online tutorials and gathering leftover fabric and textiles in the hope that the right project will come up when the time is right. 'By the time I come to tackle a new room, I have years' worth of ideas and material ready,' she says.

As such, Haines's home moves through genres, trends and atmospheres without subscribing to a particular one. 'It keeps things fluid, interesting,' she says.

The Bloomsbury-esque upcycled fireplace was hand-painted by the artist Josephine Blanchard using leftover paint samples. The plates above have been collected from charity shops over the years. The table is made from old railway sleepers. The dining chairs were bought for a "song" at £60 for 6 from Facebook Marketplace and upholstered in fabric scraps by Haines.

The sofa is an archive sofa.com model that has been in the family for 15 years and is stacked with cushions made of salvaged fabrics from Haines. The curtains and the ottoman upholstery are also from Haines. The table lamps are from Pooky's 'seconds range,' whereby surplus or damaged stock used to be sold for a lower price.

175

Jules Haines

Haines made the bed pelmet in the main bedroom by sticking fabric remnants to the front of a piece of wood she found in an antiques shop. The blue backdrop is made from a mixture of different remnants as Haines ran out of one matching design.

To incorporate a decorative version of the 'big top' for the children's bedroom, Haines made striped fabric canopies that recreated the 'tent' vibe. The handcrafted matching beds are from The Original Bed Company, in a bespoke Little Greene colour, upholstered in Haines fabric.

Peppermint tongue and groove panelling in the family bathroom is paired with
Cole & Sons leaf and snail wallpaper above. The bamboo mirror was sourced
on eBay. The fabric for the yellow blind was a remnant from Haines Collection.

Describe your style in three words.
Heritage. Colourful. Considered.

What does sustainability mean to you?
Creating something that isn't harmful to the planet. That could be because you're using something already in existence or materials that will stand the test of time. It's about being mindful of our consumption.

What are your top four tips for creating a reimagined home?
> Second-hand first.

> Considered materials always.

> Where possible, invest in craftsmanship and handmade items.

> Whenever you buy something, think about how you are going to look after it for years
  to come – it will help you avoid knee-jerk purchases.

Who or what are your inspirations in terms of sustainable design?
Edward Bulmer. I have learnt so much about colour from him. He is also my benchmark for promoting sustainability without compromising on the aesthetic.

What triggers your creativity?
Instagram. I save thousands of images that I keep on file for future decorating projects.

Your home makes you feel . . .
Grounded.

What interior item couldn't you live without?
Staple gun! It has helped create the majority of my home.

Paint colour of choice?
Jonquil by Edward Bulmer, because you can buy it in various shades and depths to fit with most decorating schemes, from a living room to a nursery.

Tell me something nobody knows about your home.
I never meant to have blue wardrobes in the bedroom. I made the mistake of choosing a colour from a chart and thought I was ordering a green shade. Luckily it works in the space, but lesson learnt – always try a paint sample before you buy.

Finish the sentence: a considered home should be . . .
Able to last generations.

A dockers' tavern reinvented
with salvaged finds

In the converted 18th-century Amsterdam tavern of Helma Bongenaar – interior stylist, author and co-founder of international lifestyle magazine *Sentimental Journal* – and Jeroen Alberts, a carpenter and artist, pieces feel like they have lived there forever.

This is an intentional vibe that Bongenaar cultivated 27 years ago, when she moved into the space with her two children (now university age but they still 'come over for dinner and a catch-up'), by kitting out the home with second-hand items and 'skip finds'. Only the sofa was bought new and that was given a Bongenaar flourish with vintage wooden legs and a bespoke gold ribbon band used as piping. Cushions made by Bongenaar from second-hand curtain remnants are scattered across the top for a lived-in vibe, reinforced by the profusion of ceramics, artworks and textiles. 'It is not necessary to buy new things,' declares Bongenaar. 'Not when there are plenty of materials that can be reused.'

When Bongenaar first moved in, only the windows and oak flooring in the living room remained intact. After its former life as a dockers' bar in the 1800s, the property was reincarnated as a shop in the 1970s, which is when a lot of the original features were lost to the renovation, and then as government-subsidized home for artists to access affordable studio space in the heart of the city. 'It soon became worn out,' explains Bongenaar. A far cry from the family home it is today.

'When people first visit, they say: "Oh, how nice that you kept all the old features", she recalls with a smile, as everything, despite being either reclaimed, second-hand or handmade by herself and Jeroen, is new to the space. The stained-glass doors came from a friend's attic down the street, which the couple picked up for free – 'everyone in the area knows that we're always on the hunt for this kind of thing' – with Jeroen adding a compact vestibule area in between the kitchen and living room from a pair of vintage school doors rescued from a skip. The kitchen flooring is made from wooden boards that Bongenaar found in a skip (much to her children's horror at the time), stripped and cut to measure. The same principle applies to an old set of doors that Bongenaar stumbled across at a building site and cut down to create kitchen cabinets. 'Jeroen and I are hands-on creatives, we thrive on the challenge of creating something new from something old,' she says.

A deep appreciation and respect for craftsmanship lies at the core of everything that Bongenaar creates. Mass-produced items are dismissed in favour of the handmade, the natural and the sustainable. 'Quick-fix products are often made out of glued wood pulp,' she says, 'which easily breaks and contributes to the waste cycle.' Each wooden panel, glass door, cupboard and reclaimed floorboard in the Bongenaar household is renewable. 'If anything breaks it can be restored or used to create something else.'

Even the paint is 'new-old', with Bongenaar mixing several leftover tester pots together to create a bespoke two-tone serene blue, based on the old colours of Amsterdam, for the kitchen cabinets. 'I was drawn to having one palette,' she says of the choice. 'One of my friends lives in Paris and every inch of her spare room is painted black. It was such a hot look in the 1980s and I was inspired by her use of one prominent colour throughout.' People often ask her the name of the paint shade, but it cannot be replicated, something that Bongenaar is quietly thankful for. 'It's the originality and the one-offness of things that makes a home special and unique.'

The same shade of blue is used to create the oval kitchen ceiling, the design of which was inspired by traditional Dutch canal houses of the 17th century. The ceilings throughout are uneven, so Bongenaar used vintage brocade instead of paint to finesse the oval outline. This design is repeated on the living room ceiling for cohesion, with the addition of old armoire panels that Bongenaar sanded and painted before screwing to the front half of the ceiling for texture. 'It's an ugly-beautiful thing that draws you into the room,' she says.

Changes made throughout the space were cosmetic rather than structural. Bongenaar rejigged the visual layout, swapping the kitchen and living room locations around. 'Growing up in the Netherlands countryside meant that when you visited a farmhouse you walked directly into the kitchen. I like that. It immediately transforms the kitchen into the heart of the home.' It's easy to see that the kitchen is Bongenaar's happy place. The dining table – sourced from a Dutch online second-hand shop and surrounded by antique Thonet chairs – is always prepped for an informal feast or coffee with friends, with Bongenaar frequently using the space to style aspirational images for her cookbooks.

Bongenaar attributes her passion for craftsmanship and salvaged gems to her childhood. Her parents were enthusiasts of the handmade and unusual, with Bongenaar spending many a weekend scouring flea markets in Belgium, France and the Netherlands in the quest for the perfect find. 'You could say it's in my DNA,' she says. Bongenaar's first personal collectible was a blue and white French ceramic bowl, which she used to drink coffee from, and she has since amassed a treasure trove of over a hundred that she mixes and matches. They currently take pride of place in a glass display cabinet in the kitchen – another 'skip gem'.

'I don't believe in wasting materials,' she says. Above the dining table in the kitchen hangs a unique chandelier decorated with 'seemingly worthless' spoons that Bongenaar found on the street. The chandelier itself is made from five different parts found at thrift shops and junk yards that Bongenaar put together and added her own fringing and spoon collection to. In the living room, curtains are made from second-hand silk scarves – one of which is a vintage Dior that Bongenaar bought for two euros at a flea market – collected over several years. Meanwhile, the guest bed was found on the street and given a Bongenaar finishing touch with old cupboard doors installed underneath as storage. In the main bedroom, bedding and pelmets were made by Bongenaar out of antique fabrics collected over the years. 'Everything I collect is old, so in that sense, it never goes out of fashion or dates,' she says.

Despite abundant collectibles, Bongenaar's outlook on furnishing her home isn't centred on striving for more. Anything that the pair no longer have space for is given to charity or rehomed, with Bongenaar regularly hosting a flea-market set up from her kitchen, which locals and tourists visit in their droves. Nothing here is a knee-jerk purchase or throwaway. Every choice is led by the heart, creating a home that prioritizes personality, not perfection.

The second hand dining table was sourced online and is often used for Bongenaar's supper clubs and cookbook shoots. The mismatched dining chairs are antique Thonet with upholstered seat cushions made by Bongenaar from old blankets hand-tied together. The original pine wood flooring has been stripped back and painted pale blue to match the cabinetry.

The kitchen cabinet that houses Bongenaar's first collection of French coffee bowls. It is her most cherished collection, featuring over 100 different designs, ranging between 50-100 years old. The cabinet was found in a skip and given a fresh coat of paint.

Bongenaar's collection of design magazines that she has contributed to over the years as a stylist. The wooden drawers were found discarded on the street and now contain Bongenaar's smaller treasures and collections.

Describe your style in three words.
Clustercore. Sentimental. Original.

What does sustainability mean to you?
Rebelling against throwaway culture and shopping reclaimed.

What are your top four tips for creating a reimagined home?
> Combine old items that span different decades throughout the house. Choose one colour to unite the scheme.

> Start a collection based on your passions, experiences and background. It's fun to collect and will make your home look and feel unique.

> Inherited an 'ugly' cupboard from your grandmother? Don't throw it away or hide it. Repurpose or repaint. It will keep the memory alive and give your home character.

> Before throwing something away, ask yourself: if I put it anywhere else, will it work better? Can I use it for something else? Or can I make someone else I know happy with it?

Who or what are your inspirations in terms of sustainable design?
The eco-art movement of the late 20th century, when artists used recycled materials and nature within their creations.

What triggers your creativity?
The holiday home we had in the south of France during the seventies; the colours of the landscape and simple style of rural housing. There was never much money to fix up houses, which brought with it an incredible charm and authenticity.

Your home makes you feel . . .
Joyous.

What interior item couldn't you live without?
My bowls. Being my first collection, they mean so much to me.

Paint colour of choice?
Soft blue, like my kitchen.

Tell me something nobody knows about your home.
Many assume that the decor is 'thrown together', but a lot of work and research went into sourcing pieces that look like they are part of the original space.

Finish the sentence: a considered home should be . . .
Somewhere you feel at your best.

As we enter a time where less is more, quality wins over quantity and it is better not to buy anything at all than the wrong thing for our homes, the desire for handcrafted items, considered collections and authentic pieces continues to rise. Where artisan and vintage finds were once considered a 'stuffy', intimidating purchase, they have since become synonymous with an appreciation for craft and the desire to support independent makers and manufacturers with green credentials, while also becoming more informed about a product's integrity in the process.

Traditional production techniques such as hand-thrown ceramics, woven rugs and hand-printed textiles, although slower to create, are continuing to make a resurgence, becoming increasingly favoured over homogeneous, mass-produced pieces that are more toxic to the environment and less likely to stand the test of time.

When everything is new, a room can feel like it has been plucked from a catalogue, whereas adding contrast with vintage, second-hand and inherited pieces will make a space feel authentic and unique to you. Think unexpected mixes of genre, pattern, shape and material, such as a Zellige tile splashback behind a shiny stainless-steel sink, or a traditional 19th-century painting displayed in a modern kitchen. Add to this the thrill of the hunt and immense satisfaction at discovering something unique and extraordinary for your home; giving new life to something that would otherwise be chucked away, often while also saving money in the process.

Such is the case in the Margate home of an interior designer, where a beloved pink sink sourced from eBay for £15 was stored for years while she saved for what became her first apartment. Likewise, in the Bali home of a photographer, where walls and surfaces are adorned with locally made items either designed by her or sourced from antique markets.

Although it isn't always convenient to shop in this way, and buying something new should not be villainized, small changes do add up. If you do find something new that you love, try to source it second-hand before buying. Supplement new pieces with elements that are reclaimed or repurposed, or, if that is not possible, make the new item a staple of your collection to bring joy for years to come.

The result will be worth it.

Conscious Sourcing

The 16th-century hall reimagined
with second-hand treasures

There isn't a single room in the home of interior designer and stylist Hannah Ellis, her husband Aled and their two children, which does not feature a second-hand or salvaged item. Tucked away on the edge of a village near Chester, their home – half of a hall that dates to the 1500s – is made up of layers of the old, the interesting and the understated.

From a framed magazine clipping Ellis found on eBay of the hall for sale in 1954, when it was first split into two halves, to the repurposed glass-fronted bookcase in the 'Smoking Room', which originally hailed from the courts in Salford before Ellis found it on Facebook Marketplace, sentiment plays a vital role in all of her design considerations. 'The house is full of things I want to be surrounded by,' she says. 'I think it's good to interact with items in a physical way – to hold them in your hand, to see the story behind them.'

Indeed, the Grade II-listed building has seen many fascinating reincarnations over the years, including as a hall for the Goldsmith of Chester during the 16th century, a base for the American army during the Second World War and home to a prestigious tailor who serviced royalty. Ellis's half of the hall was eventually carved up into separate flats in the 1960s before being reconverted to a single space in the 1980s. It is currently an amalgamation of the previous servants' quarters and a section of the original manor house.

Clues as to the hall's past lives are displayed and ingrained throughout. In the kitchen, an original Milners safe from 1920 that Ellis unearthed from under many layers of paint during the renovation sits alongside timber beams that display taper burn marks dating back to the 16th and 17th centuries and were originally believed to protect the house from evil spirits. 'Builders would have scorched the wood deliberately for good luck back then,' explains Ellis. Token remnants of previous habitations are also presented in a museum-like cabinet in Ellis's hallway and range from vintage milk bottle tops to chocolate wrappers and luggage tags dating back to the 1940s.

Despite the heritage, Ellis has been careful to steer clear of the 'ye olde' vibe typical of many 16th-century structures. The landing arch is painted in an enveloping rich gold that creates a focal point, with saturated tones of olive and chocolate slicing through the soft pink accents so that the overall look isn't 'too sugary'. Stripes are used as a leitmotif throughout on walls, alcoves and furnishings to punctuate, accentuate and zone areas. 'Stripes are nothing new, but it's about how you use them, the placement,' she says.

This is a considered renovation in which eye-catching colour choices, natural materials and patina-rich textures take centre stage. The decoration of the kitchen, for example – nicknamed 'French Fancy' due to the pale pink and honey yellow combo reminiscent of the famous cupcakes – revolves around a vintage haberdashery unit found on eBay and repurposed as a kitchen island. The teak top is an old science-lab worktop that Ellis had chopped up – the offcuts have since been used as shelves and window frames throughout – or fitted with quartzite, 'to make a stellar chopping board'. The kitchen counter worktop is an offcut of the same slab. If you look closely enough at the unit you can still see the holes where the Bunsen burners would have been placed and the gold speckles in the quartzite. 'It's like living in an evolving time capsule,' she says.

The family moved into the hall in 2019, just before the pandemic struck. The space had previously been owned by an older couple and felt dated. 'They had their renovation heyday with the hall when they first moved in, so there were obvious signs of old carpets and things that had once been great but were now not suitable,' recalls Ellis. Coming from a family of builders and growing up in the thick of the dust of one home renovation after another – Ellis was mixing cement by the age of 10 – she was no stranger to reinventing a home. Luckily there was no big renovation needed here. 'It isn't the sort of house where you strip everything back to redo it; we wanted to work with what we had where possible,' she says.

Apart from knocking through the wall that separated the kitchen and dining area to make one cohesive open-plan space, Ellis kept the pre-existing 1930s-style ceiling in the living area and lent into the contrast between the home's timeworn Jacobean-style fireplace, Victorianesque wood panelling in the Smoking Room and 1900s-era golden-brown parquet floors. The original pine-panelled doors lead to an early 19th-century staircase that has been modernized with a chocolate brown gloss to create a 'runner' effect. 'It was a durable alternative to buying carpet,' says Ellis. The original turned balusters and authentic S-shaped tread-ends are also still intact. 'My style is about honouring the past while also embracing the present and looking towards the future,' she says.

The pantry, featuring original tiled pillars and slate slab used as a worktop, is a case in point, with Ellis's collection of vintage jars and canisters collected over years from antiques fairs, charity shops and Instagram sellers, given a contemporary edge when paired with brass fittings, framed slogan tea towel and a whimsical lobster print. It strikes the interesting balance between utility and grandeur that can be seen throughout.

Ellis has always had a passion for sourcing the old, interesting and understated. A passion that has resulted in three-quarters of the home being second-hand, with only the sofas, kitchen and bed bought new. Hero items include an antique metal mirror found online for £30 ('I've seen them go for £1,000'), which involved Ellis driving to a service station in the mountains of North Wales to collect it, the French farmhouse-style dining table sourced from a vintage seller on Instagram, the Persian rug from eBay, the piano wedding gift from Ellis's husband, another eBay find, and the butcher's block repurposed as a rustic home bar in the Smoking Room, topped with whiskey and champagne dating back to the couple's wedding day. The leather armchair is from an Instagram seller.

'If grey, shiny, new products were the north pole. I would be sitting on the top of the flag on the south pole,' she smiles.

This inspirational mix of different genres embodies exactly the kind of creative exploration that Ellis seeks to capture, not only in her home but in her blossoming design business, Homespun, where she hosts design consultations, workshops and creative retreats focused on writing, painting and wellness within the space. 'My home has been such a source of inspiration to me, I hope that it will spark the beginning of a special journey for others.'

Ellis repurposed a vintage haberdashery unit from eBay as a hard-wearing kitchen island, topped with an old science-lab worktop. It multifunctions as a storage unit for recipe and design books. The bar stools were an Etsy find and needed to be glued back together. Ellis painted them in a vibrant tomato shade called 'Hearts' by eco paint brand Tikkurila.

The other half of the living room that leads into the dining area. The console is from a local antiques warehouse. Artwork throughout consists of pieces from Facebook Marketplace, Instagram sellers and antique shops from Ellis's travels to Copenhagen. The large abstract canvas painting is one of Ellis's favourite pieces that she found on Facebook Marketplace for £30. The French farmhouse oak dining table is vintage from an Instagram seller that Ellis sanded down and paired with mix and match French cafe-style chairs from various Instagram sellers and Facebook Marketplace.

When the original carpets were pulled up, raw floorboards with dark red 'tar-esque' paint marks were revealed around the perimeter of the room where the previous inhabitants had painted around the carpet to save on costs. Ellis sanded these markings back and painted over. The bed is from Loaf with Ellis working on plans to reupholster the headboard. The artwork above the bed was painted by Ellis using leftover simple paints.

Ellis hand-painted the gold scalloped wall design in her daughter's room. The pegboard featured in Ellis's son's room is designed by Ellis and custom-made by a local woodturner. It is used to store and display his rotating collection of toys.

Describe your style in three words.
Soulful. Storytelling. Trend-averse.

What does sustainability mean to you?
It's about keeping things that could serve a future purpose.

What are your top four tips for creating a reimagined home?
> Listen to the house and its history. Dive into it. Understand who lived there before. Identify them. Find their occupations. Breathe in your surroundings and feel the energy the house brings.

> Don't underestimate the power of paint; it can transform a space and modernize a traditional building.

> Shop small and second-hand. Think thrift shops, antique fairs, markets and boot sales. Second-hand furniture and artwork are so much cheaper and usually come with a story of the previous owners.

> Brown furniture. It sounds a bit old and a bit 'bleurgh', but it grounds a room and acts as a foil to more colourful elements. I have a piece of brown furniture in every room.

Who or what are your inspirations in terms of sustainable design?
Places such as Facebook Marketplace, which have made sustainable sourcing so much easier. It saves pieces from landfill, and you can often find treasures for bargain prices in the process.

What triggers your creativity?
Creativity always happens in everything; when I'm cleaning my teeth, in the shower or driving the car.

Your home makes you feel . . .
Fortunate and honoured to be the custodian of a building enveloped in so much history.

What interior item couldn't you live without?
I don't necessarily have one item, but I have old typography everywhere in the house. You could say I'm a bit of a collector! From old porcelain food pots to books and signage, there are so many wonderful examples dotted around our home, each that represent a memory. I couldn't live without these as I find them ridiculously interesting and inspiring.

Paint colour of choice?
I have strong urges towards varying shades of pink, green and brown. To pick just one would be like asking me to choose my favourite child. I have, however, received quite a lot of love for the Pickled Okra shade I have used several times in our home. It demonstrates a new vibe whenever the light changes; sometimes dirty and earthy, yet in other lights a vibrant zingy shade. Fun!

Tell me something nobody knows about your home.
I have never set foot in our attic as I'm not ready to uncover that space yet – one renovation step at a time!

Finish the sentence: a considered home should be . . .
A true manifestation of what you love and stand for. Don't fake it, make it yours.

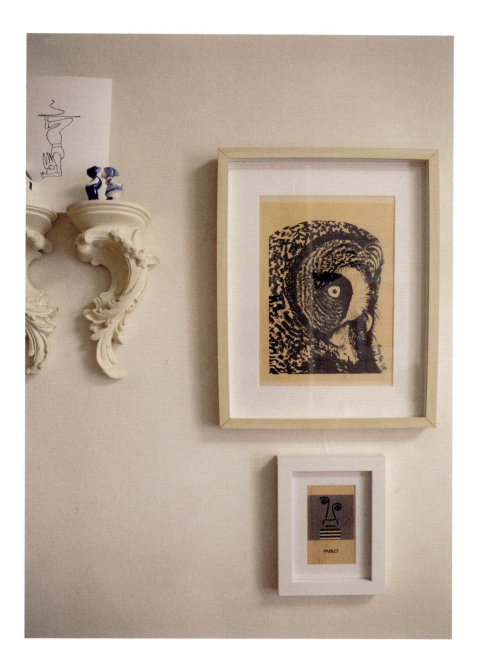

A pocket-sized chapel conversion
full of personality

Sophie van Winden has a thing for statement pieces. Growing up in a family of designers – her parents founded the flooring company First Floor ('our home had bright turquoise carpet and yellow rubber floors') – the co-founder of sustainably led interior design studio Owl already had a discerning eye for joyous jolts of colour and pattern by the time she bought her first apartment in the seaside town of Margate in 2020.

Van Winden was drawn to the unusual layout and history of the two-bedroom space. 'It was a Grade-II-listed, 200-year-old converted chapel with New York loft-living vibes,' she says. Not to mention its proximity to the beach, Margate's famous art galleries, restaurants and the humblebrag view of Tracey Emin's house from her window. 'It felt special.'

The building was carved up into 15 separate apartments in 2006, with van Winden occupying the ground floor, but still retained elements of the property's former life as a Methodist church in the form of high ceilings, thick stone walls, tall windows and floor-to ceiling metal columns. The surrounding area has many medieval crypts, with the plumbers stumbling across an old Victorian child's pram when they were underneath the floorboards sorting out the pipes. 'It was all rusted over, but still worked,' she shares.

Despite being restricted on the structural side of the renovation, van Winden added her own creative references to the building's history; a hand-painted pastel arch frames every doorway, with walls bathed in limewash for an overall monastic glow. 'I often work with daring shades and experimental palettes as part of my job,' she says, but being located on the ground floor, with no natural light in the living room – 'just really old doors that open out onto the street' – informed the decision for limewash walls over bold colour. On close inspection, the walls look 'a bit rough around the edges' – a deliberate choice by van Winden to create texture and movement throughout.

That's not to say that the palette is in any way 'vanilla'. Inspired by the dramatic sunrises and sunsets in Margate, punchy pops of pistachio and rose form the spine of the design, intermingled with accents of indigo, lilac, seafoam green and cobalt in the form of van Winden's ever-rotating kaleidoscope accessories and textiles that counterbalance the calm backdrop. 'Seen in isolation, neutral shades can look a bit greige, but here it acts as a foil for the colourful splashes,' she says.

The scheme is considered, with van Winden spending a year in the property before starting the decorative process. 'I wanted to live here for a while before changing anything,' she says. The space had not been updated since 2006. So, although the rooms were big with high ceilings, the floors were covered in 'horrible brown laminate', which made the space look even smaller. The kitchen, in particular, was a 'sea of beige cabinets', which van Winden replaced with chunky MDF in an off-white, framed by handmade ceramic tiles that span the kitchen counter and open up the space. She swapped the laminate flooring for cork in the kitchen, living room and hallway, keeping the space warm in the winter and cool during the summer months.

Due to the building's listed status, changing the compact layout wasn't an option, so van Winden leaned heavily on the transformative powers of colour and furniture to provide character. As a result, each room is an evolving showcase of preloved, vintage and contemporary finds in tactile finishes. 'I love the friction between old and new,' she says. In the living room, a vintage rug from Etsy is paired with a contemporary glass coffee table and a 1970s rattan bookshelf from eBay is laden with books inherited from her grandfather on one shelf and contemporary ceramics van Winden came across on travels or received as gifts on another. 'If you put too many vintage things together, it can look a bit fusty, and similarly, if you only have new items, schemes can lack soul,' she says.

Monochrome canvas wall hangings by sustainable Dutch brand HK Living sit above the 'eBay gold' purchase of a velvet indigo sofa by Hay, which van Winden bought for £150. Around the dining table – an archive Made.com purchase – sits a set of sought-after vintage chairs from Marcel Breuer that van Winden reupholstered in a dramatic Kravet fabric ('it goes with everything'). When paired with her vintage rose linen tablecloth, echoes the sunny scenes outside and the van Winden family holiday home in Spain. Walls provide a backdrop for her rotating art collection, comprising ceramics, canvases and paintings from independent sellers and local artists such as Studio Mond, Max Oliver and Meesh Nah, all with assorted mounts and wooden frames. 'I think home should reflect your personality,' she says. 'I'm constantly moving bits around to create little corners that bring me joy.'

There is a kinship between van Winden's knack for sourcing one-off sustainably led pieces with a sprinkling of whimsy and her day job at Owl, in which she handpicks pieces and colour schemes for clients alongside co-founder Simone Gordon. 'It's an editing process; it's about finding the right little things,' she explains. 'Even the most practical, everyday object is an opportunity to brighten your day or make you smile.' Van Winden's kitchen is a case in point, with each item the decor equivalent of a slick of red lipstick. Shell-shaped wall lights, jugs and egg holders in uplifting hues of buttercup and sage sit alongside tealight holders with fluted lids, whimsical curved vases and plates used as artwork. Even the traditional kettle has been given an Owl glow-up in pistachio green. 'Everyone needs a kettle, so why not make it a pistachio one?' It's like van Winden's version of smelling the roses.

'I like bold things, sparsely done,' she says in reference to the unapologetically pink vintage sink found on eBay for £15 (van Winden kept it for years waiting for the 'perfect space') and framed with scalloped charcoal marble tiles designed by van Winden and fabricated by Paragon Stone. The bathroom is an otherwise calm space and one that was initially van Winden's least favourite room in the apartment. 'I had to contort myself to get round the basin to the WC,' she explains. The only structural change made was to expand the bathroom into the hall, which made space for a reconfiguration and the beloved sink. 'It was all for the sink, really,' she smiles. The oval antique mirror is a souvenir from her travels to France.

The bedrooms offer a change of pace, with the original brown laminate painted white by van Winden (a budget-saving DIY project she has since grown to love), layered fabrics in gelato shades and a selection of linen cushions dyed using seaweed and food waste ('onion peel produces an amazing lilac') from van Winden's side business, Flots, where she sells sustainably made cushions and objets d'art. In the guest bedroom, a pair of chunky textured artworks found in a junk shop down the road sit above 1970s rattan headboards found on eBay. The table lamp bases are from an old Owl project, topped with second-hand shades given a playful zig-zag flourish by van Winden. In the corner sits a collection of old railway workers' lockers that van Winden repurposed as a cupboard to house her crafts and accessories.

In the main bedroom, pieces have also been picked for their narrative or history: a characterful chest of drawers from van Winden's childhood home has been given a new lease of life with concrete handles from Etsy and a lick of paint, along with vintage curved mirrors from previous Owl projects, 'I want each room to reflect memories of some kind,' she says. 'To make me smile whilst hitting the sweet spot between past and present.'

Van Winden used off-white ceramic tiles across the kitchen counters to create flow and open up the space. Limewash walls act as a foil to rotating kaleidoscopic objects including a pistachio kettle by Hay, handmade cobalt vase by ceramicist Kelly Jessiman and playful fried egg painting found in a local art shop.

The ceramic tile-clad bench swallowed most of the budget van Winden had to spend on the renovation so she incorporated storage baskets from Ikea, with locally made woven artworks from Studio Mond and paintings by Max Oliver. The previous laminate flooring throughout the kitchen, living room and hallway was replaced with cork.

Sophie van Winden

The decorative cushions are from van Winden's sustainable
side business, Flots, dyed using seaweed foraged in Margate.
The playful marshmallow-shaped bedside table is by
Polspotten. The original metal columns remain in the bedroom
and living space as a reminder of the building's history.

The guest bedroom features a pair of 1970s headboards van Winden found on eBay with papier-mâché artwork from a junk shop. The throw is from a trip to Mexico.

Describe your style in three words.
Emotive. Eye-catching. Whimsical.

What does sustainability mean to you?
Steering clear of the 'quick fix' items for ones that have longevity, without veering into 'trad' or boring.

What are your top four tips for creating a reimagined home?
> Shop small where possible. Independent sellers need your business more than the big chains and will give your home so much more character than mass-produced items.

> Try something that reminds you of a time or place in each room. I still have items from my childhood home dotted around. They bring me so much joy.

> Avoid paint with toxins, healthy walls make for a healthy home. Limewash and plaster finishes are good options.

> Reinvest back into the community by giving anything you don't want to charity shops or reclamation yards. The chances are somebody will love and rehome it.

Who or what are your inspirations in terms of sustainable design?
Sebastian Cox, a fellow Margate resident, is one of my favourite furniture designers. His handcrafted pieces are made using natural and locally sourced materials.

What triggers your creativity?
Childhood memories of sunny days spent with my dad in Spain before he passed away. The landscape and feeling of us all being together at home.

Your home makes you feel . . .
Excited.

What interior item couldn't you live without?
All the little 'bits' like my vases and art prints that make my house a home.

Paint colour of choice?
Cobalt blue is my go-to shade. It's the perfect accent colour for woodwork and for bringing drama to a compact room.

Tell me something nobody knows about your home.
It was built above a medieval crypt. My friends think it may be haunted!

Finish the sentence: a considered home should be . . .
Easy to live in and maintain.

The stateside renovation balancing
history and modernity

The juxtaposition between the dashing House of Hackney wallpaper and vintage crystal chandelier in the renovated breakfast nook of Susannah Holmberg's Salt Lake City home tells you a great deal about her taste. The space was designed by Holmberg herself as a cosy family home for husband Todd, their two children, Wyatt and Annabelle, Otto the Aussie Bernedoodle and Beatrice the chicken.

As an interior designer and one of *Architectural Digest*'s named New American Voices, Holmberg appreciates contrasting details: rough with the smooth, soft with the graphic, past with the present. The architectural shape of a contemporary block marble side table atop a hand-woven rug, a rattan floor lamp beside an abstract painting, a walnut dining table surrounded by futuristic-style chairs and an impressive collection of vintage Mexican film posters that provide bold shots of colour throughout.

'It's a real mix of the traditional and modern. A conversation starter,' she says of the twentieth-century Tudor home renovation.

Holmberg cultivated the aesthetic over time by swapping grandma-style wallpaper (it wasn't done in a 'cool' way) for paint in light-reflecting earthy tones to open up the space and dark blue carpet in the main rooms for red oak flooring, as well as accessorizing with a cornucopia of artworks and textiles to suggest a space carved out over generations. Apart from knocking through the walls – the dining room was initially separate and you had to walk through the living room to get to it, along with another doorway to get to the kitchen 'like a rabbit warren' – Holmberg used as much of the original property as possible. From structural features such as the prominent archways (resulting in the home being dubbed 'Arch House') down to all of the original handles and hardware. 'Keep old houses old,' she says. 'Embracing age and the imperfection that comes with it is beautiful.'

An unusual design philosophy for an American space to embrace: 'Properties here tend to be more on the minimal and graphic side of things,' Holmberg muses about the majority of her client design requests. But for Holmberg, who has always been intrigued by and drawn to modern flourishes in historic buildings – 'interiors should have soul, character, history,' – good design should hit the 'sweet spot' between the right amount of vintage, the right amount of refinement and mid-century pops. As such, Holmberg's style isn't very 'done', which separates her from other stateside designers. 'People tear down old houses all the time here or modernize them with new fixtures and fittings that don't work with the bones of the building. That's not my style,' she says.

Holmberg was careful not to over-modernize the space, bringing in era-appropriate details that either replicated the style of the original features or materials that would evolve over time with the space. Upon moving in, the kitchen was 'very 1990s', with an abundance of yellowed wooden cabinets, soulless white tile countertops and large ceramic floor tiles that jarred with the heritage of the property.

Holmberg replaced the cabinets with handmade flat-fronted versions that she painted in Beachwood by Portola Paints – a grey-green tone that adds a jolt of colour without dominating the space – updated the tiles with red oak flooring and the countertops with contemporary Calacatta Macchia Vecchia marble, before adding a hand-carved wooden pillar in the centre of the room, all of which create a thoughtful interplay between the old and new.

The kitchen island, wrapped in biodegradable, white-washed oak dowels to create a fluted effect, anchors the space and is Holmberg's pride and joy. 'It multifunctions as a practical area to cook and a place to entertain family and friends,' she says. Elements such as the immersive botanical wallpaper, sleek lines of the kitchen island stools and modern silhouette of the Tulip table in the adjacent breakfast nook offer contemporary contrasts without distracting from the historical references.

When it comes to the palette, Holmberg cites her travels around the sunshine-filled kitchens of Morocco and the vibrant architecture of Spain and Mexico as her springboard. Core colours of sage green, chocolate brown and oxblood are punctuated with slices of teal and repeated on various scales throughout. They feel authentic to the period of the house while also working in tandem with the more modern elements. 'There is something organic about the way they use colour in Mexico,' says Holmberg, 'like it has been naturally integrated into their lives. I'm drawn to that.'

Despite the cohesive colour thread, Holmberg has given each room its own strong identity with punchy accents – a lick of teal paint on the fireplace, a sage trim on the woodwork – and a unique collection of 1stDibs-worthy furniture pieces: mid-century, vintage and antique finds that seem to tell their own stories. In the breakfast nook, a mismatched collection of vintage Thonet bentwood dining chairs from an Etsy seller in France, in the living room a dining table that guests assume Holmberg spent 'thousands' on but was a Craigslist find and the mid-century Chilean lounge chair that was one of Holmberg's first pieces of furniture. 'I couldn't afford the shipping, so they sent it to me on the Greyhound bus,' she smiles. It hasn't left her side since. Anything that has been bought new has been on the basis that the aesthetic will transcend trends and, in time, become a classic.

The how, where and when things were made matters to Holmberg, with a strong focus on natural materials and items primarily sourced and bought locally: lambswool and cashmere rugs, earthenware pots, marble coffee tables, red and white oak flooring and practical items used in unexpected ways, such as the woven hammock repurposed and hung as a piece of artwork above Holmberg's bed. 'It's just the right amount of quirkiness,' she says.

Despite appearances, the space is not complete, however. 'Sometimes I would love to snap my fingers and have the time and money to get what my clients get, which is a finished space that they just walk into,' she reflects. 'But I also like living in an ever-evolving workshop of materials and patterns. A space that is joy-led without being precious.'

Beatrice the chicken takes a stroll around the open-plan kitchen, dining room and breakfast nook. The cabinets are made from FSC timber by Benchmark Woodwork, painted in an earthy green-grey shade with Ikea drawer pulls painted the same shade.

233

Susannah Holmberg

The dining room was previously a rabbit warren with walls and swinging saloon doors, which Holmberg opened up, recreating the original arched detail featured throughout the rest of the house. Here colours patterns and textures overlap; from a House of Hackney botanical print wallpaper, to the Craigslist find walnut dining table, hand knotted wool rug and red oak stained flooring.

Susannah Holmberg

236

A generous marble-topped coffee table from
Facebook Marketplace creates space for handmade
vessels and Holmberg's vast collection of design
books. The rug is hand-knotted wool.

The breakfast nook is adjacent to the open-plan kitchen, which Holmberg opened up by knocking down the original dividing wall. The Tulip table is second-hand. The chandelier is vintage.

Susannah Holmberg

Describe your style in three words.
Layered. Soulful. Unique.

What does sustainability mean to you?
Zero waste.

What are your four tips for creating a reimagined home?
> Understanding and respecting the lineage of spaces and items. My son is fourteen and wanted to move down to the basement to have more space and privacy. He didn't like the sofa I had down there until I told him that it was the sofa Nana bought me when I moved into my first apartment. It's part of our family history. Now he thinks it's cool.

> Invest in new pieces if they work better for your space and budget, but try to reuse where possible. These are the pieces that will make your space look and feel unique.

> Having fun with colour doesn't mean you need to always need to go bold; accent shades used in slices and slithers work just as well in the right context as a colour-drenched room.

> Focus on pieces that have craft, detail and heart at their core.

Who or what are your inspirations in terms of sustainable design?
There is a local architecture practice here, Klima, who creates beautiful and inspiring passive house projects.

What triggers your creativity?
Travel. I spent a long time in India, Nepal and Morocco and fell in love with the architecture and the use of colour there.

Your home makes you feel . . .
Happy.

What interior item couldn't you live without?
Probably the family sofa we have had for years and years.

Paint colour of choice?
I love Greenblack by Sherwin Williams. It is beautiful when you want to amp up the drama in a space without overwhelming it.

Tell me something nobody knows about your home.
To save on budget, our kitchen floor was originally plywood that was painted black. Thankfully that is no longer the case!

Finish the sentence: a considered home should be . . .
A reflection of the lives lived in it.

A Balinese shack inspired
by nature

In many ways, Nathalie Rühs's home and brand defies labels. Located in the Uluwatu region of southern Bali, it is a collection of contradictions: pared-back yet atmospheric, raw but sensuous, show-stopping yet intimate. Colour punctuates and permeates throughout in the form of Rühs's hand-painted vessels and handmade shell vases, earthy-hued upholstery and breathable limewash plaster. Nothing here is showy or statement, but presented in a natural way that resonates with her design ethos and mindful lifestyle brand, Maison Ra.

Launched by Rühs in 2021, Maison Ra is the ever-evolving art project, creative studio and home that she shares with her husband, Francisco, and their two sons, Ra and Artemis. It is the physical manifestation of Rühs's roles as interior designer, photographer and artist, from which she runs creative, sustainably led workshops ranging from clothes dyeing using native Indonesian plants to art and photography. As such, Maison Ra is a space where 'sustainability, creativity and family life converge,' explains Rühs. 'Essentially, it is an extension of us.'

For Rühs, the word 'sustainability' extends beyond a mere trend and desire for limewashed walls, however. Rather, it is a way of being, a mindset. 'Maison Ra encourages us to simplify things and foster a deeper connection to the landscape,' she says. It is also the embodiment of her passion for combatting overconsumption and waste within the interiors industry and wider world. As a former lawyer, Rühs had already carved out a name within corporate corridors, but upon moving to Bali in 2018 she was keen to embark on a new creative chapter that better reflected her values.

From teaching yoga to pottery and photography that celebrates the female form – many of Rhus's portraits are displayed throughout the house – Rühs immersed herself in various creative pursuits. These ventures, coupled with co-designing Terra Cottages, a boutique Berber-inspired hotel located on the southern peninsula, tapped into her skill for designing spaces that work in harmony with the environment. 'For me, sustainability is about cultivating a relationship with our surroundings,' she says. 'We are just as much a part of Mother Nature as she is of us.'

As Rühs points out, serendipity also played a role in the creation of Maison Ra. 'When I first arrived in Bali, I was drawn to a local coffee shack clad in reconfigured driftwood salvaged from ships. The rustic charm of it made my soul sing,' she recalls. It was there that Rühs came across an ad for a long-term rental. 'It was just a small concrete block,' she recalls. But it had driftwood ceilings that echoed the vibe of the shack. 'I just had to see it.'

As it was a rental, Rühs was in no rush to jump into an extensive renovation. It wasn't until the couple bought the space a year later that the renovation journey began. 'By then we had experienced the space, understood its nuances and how we wanted to live in it,' she says. The renovation process was a labour of love, underpinned by Rühs's hands-on approach and drive for sustainable design. 'We didn't want to rip out many existing features,' she reflects, 'but rather work with what we had, like putting together pieces of a puzzle.'

Rühs painted the original driftwood ceilings off-white and installed large sun windows throughout to maximize the light. She extended the footprint of the space by building and merging a mirror image second half of the house. 'We lived in the original half during the process', Rhus recalls. She tiled over the outdoor space – 'originally a mud bath, especially during the wet season' – in natural sandstone to further blur the lines between the indoors and out. With a view to future-proofing, Rhus also planted a fruit and vegetable garden for her growing family.

Rühs's love of nature and the handmade is evident throughout. In the kitchen, rustic wooden cupboards made from reclaimed teak wood and window shutters were designed by Rhus and made by a local carpenter – 'if you look closely you can see that the doors are a bit crooked and have gaps in between' – with a built-in concrete shelving unit in the dining room (coated in limewash) created from a simple drawing Rühs gave the local craftsmen. 'They couldn't understand why I wanted so many deliberately mismatched holes in my unit,' she muses, and the hand-carved timber doors featured throughout were made from furniture off-cuts. 'The grain does not match, but that's what gives it character.'

Tactile layers add an element of softness and enhance the natural aesthetic; organic linens in various earthy shades of tobacco, terracotta and sea green are used as throws, bed linen and tablecloths. The upholstered terracotta tub chair in the bedroom, made locally in Bali, is a recreation of a piece Rühs came across on Pinterest. 'Things here are often made to order, which cuts down on waste,' she explains. Imaginative layers of basketry and one-off handmade ceramics from Borneo further add to the decorative appeal.

Most of the pieces here are low-cost and chosen for their functionality. Namely, the weathered teak dining table, purchased by Rühs for 100 euros from a local antique dealer and 'given a spruce' and in the living room, the coffee table that multifunction's as a bench that was a gift from the carpenter who built the kitchen. 'Simplicity is key for me,' reflects Rühs. 'I prefer the lines of an uncomplicated silhouette and the imperfect knots in wood. It's these pieces that give a home joy, meaning . . . life.' She hopes that things will go full circle and that her children will one day have these pieces in their own homes.

With the studio, home and family so intertwined, it feels as if this legacy will transcend many generations to come.

In the living area, a teak wood coffee table, gifted to
Rühs by the same carpenter who built the kitchen,
multifunctions as a dining bench. The sofa is custom-
made and upholstered in a cotton linen mix.

Ruhs designed the limewash bathroom as a home birthing station for son Ra, which has since become a calming evening space for her two boys. The shutters were custom-made. The bath is made from terrazzo with the splashback and vanity unit clad in green ceramic tiles to echo the colours of the surrounding landscape. The sink is made from locally sourced marble.

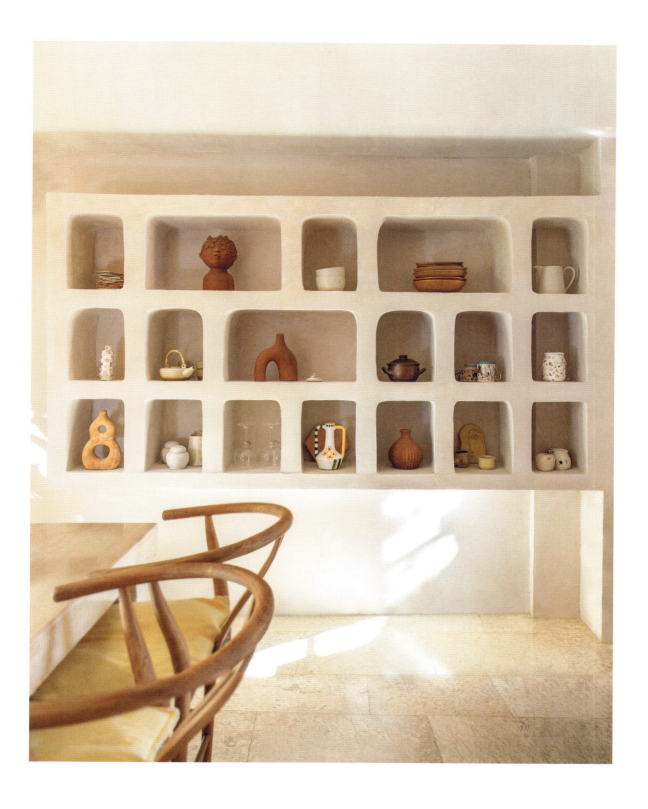

The kitchen is a simple but functional space with Rühs drawing the design for the cupboards and shutters on a piece of paper for the local carpenters to make out of reclaimed teak wood. The compact kitchen island, also designed by Rühs, is made out of travertine, with locally sourced marble tiles spanning the ground floor.

Nathalie Rühs

The bedroom has a unique doorway hand carved from furniture offcuts. Inside, the bed is swathed in organic linens, with a small Moroccan rug used as a tactile piece of art. The flooring upstairs was either recycled from old boats or made from coconut wood, an abundantly grown tree in Indonesia that helps absorb carbon.

Nathalie Rühs

Describe your style in three words.
Earthy. New-bohemian. Dreamy.

What does sustainability mean to you?
Restoring our relationship with nature.

What are your top four tips for creating a reimagined home?
› Opt for a neutral foundation in terms of colours – it acts as the perfect foil to playful pieces and bolder colours.

› Bring fun elements of nature into every corner of your home; a wood *plumeau* duster, pastel cotton mops, laundry wires hung in between the trees. It will allow you to romanticize everything, even doing the laundry.

› Steer clear of trends and only surround yourself with items that mean something to you and tell a story. I like to paint vases and cover old candle jars with plaster and seashells to display around the home. Plus, if one of the kids drops it, I can easily make another.

› Transform your home into a living museum of your life; I find a lot of joy in hanging my photography work on the walls as an evolving art project. The collection grows with our family and adjusts as we change over the years.

Who or what are your inspirations in terms of sustainable design?
People who make everything with their hands using elements and materials they found in the wild.

What triggers your creativity?
The beauty in the mundane. I especially like looking at how lighting can make seemingly inanimate objects look like they're in motion.

Your home makes you feel . . .
At peace. Content.

What interior item couldn't you live without?
My 100 per cent linen bed sheets. They remind me of my time spent in Europe.

Paint colour of choice?
Limewash in earthy tones.

Tell me something nobody knows about your home.
It used to belong to a German surfboard designer. He made the boards in a workshop to the side of the house.

Finish the sentence: a considered home should be . . .
Like your favourite novel: familiar, welcoming and nourishing for the soul.

Acknowledgements

Creating this book has been an honour and privilege, made even more special by the team of creatives around me, who supported me and believed in the journey. I have found your stories compelling, passion-inspiring and your abundant creativity infectious. Working with you all has made the book for me and I cannot thank you enough for allowing me into your personal worlds and sharing snippets of your lives.

A huge thank you to Simon Bevan for his captivating photography and ability to translate the message of *The Reimagined Home* through the lens. It has been so much fun working with you on this project. I also couldn't have created this book without the help of Ian Tillotson, Laura Hart and Isla Doran, whose attention to detail, talent, humour and thorough understanding of the project helped make this book what it is.

And, of course, a big thanks to all the contributing photographers: Jade Sarkhel, French + Tye, Matthew Williams, Derek Swalwell, Sue Stubbs, Helma Bongenaar, Martina Gemmola, Jennifer Soo, and Malissa Mabey, who have taken such beautiful images for this project. Thank you for all of your hard work and dedication.

A huge thanks to all the team at Penguin, in particular Kate Pollard and Eve Marleau for all their excitement and guidance and for giving me the opportunity to create this book. Also, to my editor Hannah Boursnell, who took my words and gave them wings. It's been a joy to work on this project together.

To Vaughan Mossop, who has created beautifully designed pages and has really embraced the vision of this project.

To my family: my beautiful children, Autumn and Oisín, who are a constant course of inspiration to me, my brilliant husband Thom, without whose support this journey would not have begun, and my parents, Christine and Liam, for always encouraging me to cut my own creative path.

Lastly, thanks to everyone who came on this journey with me and picked up a copy of this book. I can't tell you what it means to me and how much I appreciate your support. I hope it inspires you to reimagine a home you love.

About the Author

Nicole Gray is a UK-based interiors stylist, art director, writer and creative consultant. Curious about people and passionate about creating visuals and words that bring to life spaces, stories and brands, she has spent the past fifteen years working with established global companies, smaller start-ups and international magazine titles. Her work has been featured in prestigious interiors magazines and newspapers including *Elle Decoration*, *Livingetc*, *Red*, the *Telegraph* and *The Times*. Nicole frequently collaborates with leading photographers and her work has been syndicated internationally in *Domino* and *Real Living*.

Quadrille, Penguin Random House UK, One Embassy Gardens, 8 Viaduct Gardens, London SW11 7BW

Quadrille Publishing Limited is part of the Penguin Random House group of companies whose addresses can be found at global. penguinrandomhouse.com

Penguin Random House UK

Copyright © Nicole Gray

Nicole Gray asserted his right to be identified as the author of this Work in accordance with the Copyright, Designs and Patents Act 1988

Published by Quadrille in 2025

www.penguin.co.uk

A CIP catalogue record for this book is available from the British Library

ISBN 978-1-78488-969-2
10 9 8 7 6 5 4 3 2 1

Publishing Director: Kate Pollard
Designer: Vaughan Mossop, Daniel New
Copy editor: Hannah Boursnell
Proofreader: Michela Parkin
Photographers: Simon Bevan, Derek Swalwell (p10–26), Sue Stubbs (p44–56), French + Tye (p58–70), Jade Sharkhel (p74–90, p242–254), Martina Gemmola (p104–118), Matthew Williams (p92–102), Helma Bongenaar (p184–194), Malissa Mabey (p228–240)
Production Director: Stephen Lang
Production Manager: Sabeena Atchia

Colour reproduction by p2d
Printed in China by C&C Offset Printing Co., Ltd.

The authorised representative in the EEA is Penguin Random House Ireland, Morrison Chambers, 32 Nassau Street, Dublin D02 YH68.

Artwork credits

P48 Colourful abstract painting on partition wall: Sally Scales
P49/50 Orange artwork of bowl on living room wall: Yaritji Heffernan
P49/50 Bunnies print on gallery wall: Paul Worstead
P49/50 Fruit bowl painting on gallery wall: Anna May Henry
P50 Blue ceramic plate on gallery wall: Zaachariaha Fielding
P51 Sketch watercolour of female: Paul Worstead
P56 Roadway photo behind shelley: Alan Lippert
P69 print: Andreas Gursky
P85 Lime green painting with birds: Budi
P89 Portrait of young boy: Filippo Sciascia
P113 Dot painting: Sara Willett
P115 Woman washing: Karen Goodall
P128 'I'm in the bushes' print: Babak Ganjei
P147 Canvas artwork: Hannah Noble
P168 Corkscrew shrimp: Tommy Penton
P174/175 Paper mache stag head: Michael Methven
P207 Abstract painting: Facebook Marketplace/Artist unknown
P213 Abstract painting: Facebook Marketplace/Artist unknown
P214 Canvas wall hangings; HK Living/Artist unknown
P214 Architecture artwork: Alfred Waterhouse
P215 Owl print: Minnie Mae Stott
P215 Abstract postcard underneath: Picasso
P219 Pink artwork above the console in the hallway: Meesh Nah
P220 Pastel framed prints: Charlotte Taylor
P221 Woven artworks: Studio Mond
P221 Small apple painting: Max Oliver
P222 Pink artwork above the bed: Meesh Nah
P228 Hammock: Coqui Coqui
P233 Abstract painting: Carol Crain
P234 Monochrome portrait: Andrew Alba
P238 Abstract painting: Miro Lithograph
P239 Framed film posters: Vintage/artists unknown